KEYS TO ADOPTING A CHILD

Kathy Lancaster, M.A.

BARRON'S

Cover photo by Scott Barrow, Inc., Cold Spring, NY

© Copyright 1994 by Barron's Educational Series, Inc.

All rights reserved.
No part of this book may be reproduced in any form, by photostat, microfilm, xerography, or any other means, or incorporated into any information retrieval system, electronic or mechanical, without the written permission of the copyright owner.

All inquiries should be addressed to:
Barron's Educational Series, Inc.
250 Wireless Boulevard
Hauppauge, New York 11788

Library of Congress Catalog Card No.: 94-5222

International Standard Book No. 0-8120-1925-3

Library of Congress Cataloging-in-Publication Data
Lancaster, Kathy
    Keys to adopting a child / Kathy Lancaster.
      p. cm.
    Includes bibliographical references (p.   ) and index.
    ISBN 0-8120-1925-3
    1. Adoption—United States. II. Title. III. Series
HV875.55.L35 1994   94-5222
362.7'33'0973—dc20   CIP

PRINTED IN THE UNITED STATES OF AMERICA
4567   5500   98765432

CONTENTS

	Introduction: Adoption for a 21st Century Family	vi
	Part One—Making the Decision to Adopt	**1**
1	Accepting Infertility	3
2	The Decision to Adopt	8
3	Support Systems	13
	Part Two—Why Is Adopting a Child So Difficult?	**18**
4	Supply and Demand	20
5	Adoption Laws: "Best Interest of the Child"	22
	Part Three—Changes in Adoption Practices	**25**
6	Movement Toward Openness	27
7	Expanding Options	30
8	Who Can Adopt?	33
	Part Four—Who Can Be Adopted?	**35**
9	Domestic White Infants	36
10	International Children	38
11	Children of Color	41
12	Children in Interim Care	43
13	Waiting Children	46
	Part Five—Styles of Adoption	**49**
14	Agency or Independent?	51
15	Confidential, Semiopen, or Open?	55
16	Domestic or International?	58

Part Six—The Legal Process of Adoption — **60**
17 Regulations and Procedures — 61
18 Jurisdiction, Interstate, and International Adoptions — 65
19 Safeguards for a Successful Adoption — 68

Part Seven—Planning an Adoption Strategy — **75**
20 A Six-Step Plan — 76
21 Choosing an Adoption Professional — 80
22 Staying Actively Involved — 85
23 Risks and Stresses — 88

Part Eight—Locating a Birthmother on Your Own — **90**
24 Parent-Initiated Adoption — 92
25 Advertising for Birthparents — 96
26 Networking — 102
27 Flyers — 104
28 Mailings — 107
29 Classified Advertising — 110
30 Advertising Successes and Failures — 118
31 Initial Communications with Birthparents — 121
32 Keys to a Successful Match — 127

Part Nine—Building a Family Through Adoption — **132**
33 Family Preparation — 134
34 Easing the Child's Transition — 138
35 Insurance, Benefits, and Subsidies — 141

Part Ten—Beyond the Process of Adoption — **144**
36 Bonding and Entitlement — 146
37 Coping with Disappointment — 150
38 Speaking Positively About Adoption — 154
39 A True Story for Nontraditional Adopters — 157

Questions and Answers	169
Glossary	172
Suggested Reading	178
Appendix A: Adoption Organizations	181
Appendix B: State Adoption Agencies	184
Index	191

INTRODUCTION: ADOPTION FOR A 21ST CENTURY FAMILY

The good news in modern adoption is that as a prospective adoptive parent, you have many options. Contrary to what you may have heard about the roadblocks to adopting a child, the opposite is quite true. You can be successful in adopting just the right child to fit into your family.

You have choices about the type of child you would like to adopt, the degree of confidentiality involved in the adoption, your selection of an adoption professional, and a game plan to follow in pursuing your adoption. If you are a nontraditional adopter—single, gay or lesbian, from a racial or religious minority, older, or physically challenged—you have an opportunity to be evaluated on your potential to love and nurture a child rather than your ability to fit neatly into a "perfect parent" profile.

Fortunately for all members of the adoption circle—adopted children, birthparents, and adoptive parents—fixed rules about adoption no longer apply. The old attitudes about who can adopt and how an adoption is supposed to proceed are being replaced by adoptions that are individualized to suit the key people involved.

INTRODUCTION: ADOPTION FOR A 21ST CENTURY FAMILY

The state of adoption in the United States has been altered dramatically in recent years. Some of these revisions reflect a changed society. Others are the result of courts and legislatures taking a closer look at the welfare of children. Still others have sprung from the work of grass roots adoption advocates who fervently believe that adoption works.

Children's Rights

Two major influences are guiding legislative and judicial activities related to children and modern adoption: (1) a belief that all children deserve a permanent home, and (2) a principle known as the "best interest of the child." As a result, children's rights have become an important consideration in the formulation of new laws and in legal interpretations in court cases. Efforts have been made to move children through the legal system more quickly to avoid lengthy stays in interim care, and in many cases, when conflicts arise, the rights and the welfare of children are being weighed more heavily than the custody rights of their parents.

Increased Communication Between Birth and Adoptive Parents

A striking change in modern adoption is the practice of increased communication between birthparents and adoptive parents. Often, birthparents and prospective adopters are meeting and making decisions together about the future of a child about whom they all care deeply.

This idea of allowing a degree of communication between birth and adoptive parents has greatly changed the traditional cloistered picture of adoption in the United States. Adoption policies and procedures in the middle of this century were built on the belief that everyone benefited from secrecy in adoption. Today, many believe that a measure of communication is vitally important, even if the communication amounts to nothing more than access to the medical history of the adopted child.

Although confidential adoption continues to be a popular choice for some adopters and birthparents, increased communication—often an exchange of nonidentifying information—serves adopted children, who benefit from access to their medical and social records and, frequently, letters and mementos from their birthparents.

Active Involvement by Birth and Prospective Adoptive Parents

In most states, birthmothers have the right to choose adoptive parents for their children. They may choose from agency profiles of couples wishing to adopt. They may respond to newspaper advertisements submitted by prospective adopters. They may even advertise themselves and make the choice completely free of interference from adoption agencies. The only requirement is compliance with their state adoption laws. (If the birthparents and adoptive parents reside in different states, the laws of each state must be considered and the adoption must comply with the Interstate Compact on the Placement of Children. See Key 18.)

In many states and some foreign countries, prospective adoptive parents are becoming actively involved in locating birthparents on their own rather than waiting for agency workers to match them with a child. Prospective adoptive parents are using adoptive parent support groups and their own networking systems and are mounting successful advertising campaigns to expand their options and locate adoptable children.

Wider Array of Adoptive Parents

Biologically built families are parented by married couples, older parents, singles, gays and lesbians, physically challenged parents, and parents whose race or religion differs from that of their children. Increasingly, the makeup of adoptive families reflects this diversity. Although the vast majority of adopters continue to be married couples, other prospective parents are gaining an opportunity to adopt as well. The ability to love and nurture a child and the sincere desire "just to be Mom or Dad" weigh heavily in a prospective adoptive parent's favor.

Some adoptions are assisted by adoption professionals who specialize in placing children with nontraditional adopters. In other cases, nontraditional adopters are forming their own adoptive parent support groups. Members serve as their own resource and networking systems to help others who would like to adopt.

Increased Emphasis on Preserving a Child's Cultural Heritage

Many adoption professionals and adult adoptees believe that adopted children do best when they are encouraged to examine and take pride in their personal, biological heritage. This sense of personal history is a strong element in the development of any child's self-esteem and is especially critical for a child who may look different from his family or friends.

Realizing the importance of building self-esteem in their children, many adoptive parents are encouraging their children's pride in their heritage. They accomplish this by (1) speaking with the child about her heritage, (2) sharing books and information about the child's culture and customs, (3) providing opportunities for contact with other children or adults of the child's ethnic origin, and (4) joining support groups with families of similar diversity.

Information about biological parents is particularly helpful in building this pride in cultural heritage and, as such, is a strong argument in favor of providing children with information about their backgrounds.

Rights for Adoptive Families

Adoptive families have lobbied for fair and equal treatment on a variety of social issues. Such groups have made inroads in equal rights to health insurance coverage, family leave privileges, and access to records and services. Although discrepancies remain, the efforts of these lobbying groups have brought the rights of adoptive families to the forefront and changes toward equity have been meaningful.

An especially significant change has been in expanded health care coverage for adopted children whose parents receive health care coverage from employers. (See Key 35.)

Use of Positive Adoption Language

Although adoption practices have changed dramatically in recent years, public perception about adoption has not changed significantly. In an attempt to change this public perception, adoption advocates have developed what they term positive adoption language (PAL).

Positive adoption language is an unemotional, nonjudgmental expression of the practices and policies of adoption. Through PAL, advocates hope to dispel myths about adoption, including stereotypes about birthparents and their reasons for choosing adoption, and to replace these myths with accurate information about adopted children, birthparents, and adoptive families.

By using positive adoption language, we can all help to shape society's attitudes about adoption and, in doing so, positively influence the lives of adopted children. The use of positive adoption language can be a powerful tool for helping people become sensitive to adoption issues and helping adopted children understand their rightful place in society. (See Key 38 for a discussion of positive adoption language.)

Continuing Advances

As a result of the combined voices of adoption proponents, children's advocates, and affinity groups, such as adoption support groups, changes are being made for the benefit of children and the equity of families built through adoption.

Yes, it is true that families built through adoption are different. Children may look different from their adoptive parents. They may have memories of another family or families with whom they shared their lives before joining their new families. They certainly joined their adoptive families in a different way from the way many children joined their families.

Yet, adoption advocates do not hesitate to stress the similarities between adoptive and biologically built families. Families are families. There are absentee fathers and absentee mothers, big kids and little kids, and in-between kids.

Families in the twenty-first century will reflect diversity. What is important is that kids have homes and moms and dads who love and care for them.

As a prospective adopter, you have a wealth of new options. Do not allow misconceptions or previous discouragements to keep you from experiencing and enjoying parenting.

Do not sell yourself short, either. You have a unique personality and life-style to offer a child. Somewhere there really is a child who fits exactly into this life. Neither should you compromise on what you really want from the experience based on what you may have heard are your only options.

All sorts of people can be wonderful parents, and all sorts of kids can be wonderful children. Whether you choose to parent a domestic infant, an international child, a special needs child, or a child who has been a part of the interim care system, there is a place for you in adoption today.

However, and this is very important, do not pursue the adoption of an international or special needs child, or a child who has been a part of the interim care system because you may succeed more quickly. Adoption involves a lifetime commitment. Although placement may come quickly, you must be prepared for the challenges presented by the individual child whom you choose to parent.

Adoption can truly be the best of all worlds, a situation that serves children, birthparents, and adoptive parents. It is up to you to make some key decisions and become active in accomplishing an adoption plan. And, yes, you truly will be able to adopt the child you want.

Part One

MAKING THE DECISION TO ADOPT

The decision to build all or part of your family through adoption frequently comes after a personal struggle with infertility or with the realization that your social status—being single, for instance—will impede you from conceiving a child. Although some choose to expand their biologically built family through adoption, most adopters wish to adopt to fulfill a personal need rather than through a desire to help society.

The days when families "took in" an orphaned or abandoned child in need of a home are gone along with the orphan trains of the late 1800s. You may of course choose to adopt a particular waiting child who pulls at your heartstrings, but in essence most adopters choose adoption to satisfy their desire to parent.

Adoption professionals caution prospective adopters to consider their motives for adoption carefully. They also urge infertile couples to come to grips with their infertility before making the decision to adopt. Even then, the professionals caution, adoption is not merely the next step after acceptance of infertility. Infertile couples have several options: adoption is one of them.

If you are infertile, you must examine all your choices. You must also deal with the losses that infertility brings.

Only then can you accept an adopted child for who she is, rather than as a replacement for the child you are unable to conceive.

If you are single you must also consider your ability to parent a child in a single-parent household. Do you have the physical, emotional, and financial resources to parent a child? Do you, for example, have a strong support system—parents or friends nearby—who can help when you are called out of town, are sick, or just need an evening to yourself? Do you have access to friends or family members who can serve as opposite sex role models and gender balancers for your child?

If you are a fertile couple who wish to expand your family through adoption, carefully consider your motives for adoption. Families built through adoption bring their own sets of challenges. Few will applaud you for your humanitarian service of parenting another person's child. Your dedication must be to provide a loving and stable environment to the children you parent through adoption as well as those you parent biologically.

The decision to adopt has broad effects. Not only does adoption affect you, the adoptive parent, but it affects your child, your child's birthparents, and the extended families of both birth and adoptive parents. Adoption is a decision that lasts a lifetime.

1

ACCEPTING INFERTILITY

The vast majority of prospective adopters are infertile, yet adoption is not a panacea for couples facing the disappointment of permanent infertility. Adoption provides the opportunity to parent, an opportunity that infertility takes away. For some prospective adopters, being a mom or a dad is all they wish for and adoption can give them this opportunity. For others, the loss of a flesh-and-blood connection to future generations is an important issue that adoption cannot remedy.

If you are in the early stages of confronting your infertility, you are probably finding out that modern fertility treatments have become sophisticated, extensive, and expensive. For many couples, there is an almost endless variety of new techniques and treatments. Others face the grim reality of permanent infertility early in their treatment.

A couple undergoing infertility treatment has several options they may choose to examine anytime during treatment. If you are currently receiving treatment that is proving to be unsuccessful, you may be examining your options right now. These options include the following:

- Continue infertility treatment (up to and including exhausting all possibilities of treatment)

- Use donated eggs or sperm to conceive a child and thus retain a genetic connection to the child
- Adopt
- Maintain a life-style without children

Your choice from among these options will be guided by four elements: your own and your partner's goals for parenting, your intended life-style, your finances, and your energy and stress levels. Each option involves decisions and consequences. Continuation of treatment may strain your finances and your emotions, only to result in the conclusion of "no more treatments, no more options." Assisted reproduction, such as donor insemination, egg donation, or surrogacy, can provide a genetic link to the fertile partner. The choice carries an element of isolation for the nonfertile partner, however. Adoption may be a lengthy process that is straining both emotionally and financially, particularly after the stresses of infertility treatments. And although the decision to be child free finalizes all the choices, it allows you to place infertility behind you and to embrace your chosen life-style.

If you have decided to accept your infertility as permanent—that is, to stop treatment and move on to one of the other three options—it is important that you also understand and accept the losses that infertility brings to your life. Unresolved infertility issues can linger throughout your life and interfere with future life choices.

Adoption professionals warn prospective adopters that unresolved infertility losses are likely to interfere with complete acceptance of an adopted child. You may, they believe, subconsciously hold the same expectations for a child who enters your family through adoption as for a child born to you. Can you, for example, be entirely sure that you can accept your adopted child's interest in mechanics (or art or drama) over an ambition to attend college?

Because many couples have not experienced infertility—and those who do often keep their experiences private—the losses of infertility are minimized by society. How often have you heard, "Just relax and it will work when you quit trying so hard," or, "Well, you can always adopt. That's the easy way, anyway!" Infertile couples are often left to cope with their losses on their own. You struggle with the promise of "just one more treatment," and failing that, you often lack information and help about how to move on with your life.

Infertile couples are often not aware that the infertility has brought them face to face with a major loss in life. Some infertile couples who have acknowledged the loss equate it with the silent mourning for a child lost through miscarriage, an event for which there is no societal ceremony in which the mourners can share their sorrow and grieve their loss.

The most obvious loss in infertility is the loss of a genetic connection. Without a biologically conceived child, no one will carry on your genetic traits. No little girl will have your smile; no little boy will share your gift for music. Of course, even a biologically conceived child is no guarantee of a continuance of these traits, but with infertility the loss is guaranteed.

A second loss that infertility brings is the loss of control. As an infertile couple, you lose the ability to decide the timing of your children and the number of children you will have. You even lose the opportunity to decide for yourself whether you will be a suitable parent. Yes, you do have choices in which fertility treatments to pursue and which surgeries or procedures to try. Despite the access to modern technologies, though, when you reach the last of the choices, you have nothing else to try. No amount of persuasion can change this.

A third, related loss that accompanies infertility is the loss of privacy. If you have experienced infertility treatments, you know that the most intimate areas of your private life are scheduled, microscopically examined, and evaluated by teams of health care professionals. In addition, you face the curiosity of well-meaning friends and family, who are wondering, "Just what is taking so long to get pregnant?" If you decide to adopt, you face the further scrutiny of yet another team of professionals who are empowered to make decisions about your suitability to parent a child.

An opportunity to create a child jointly—complete with his athletic ability and her talent for math—is yet a fourth loss to infertile couples. What newly married couple doesn't fantasize about the beautiful children they will conceive? This is a natural part of life, love, and family building.

Fifth, infertile couples lose the opportunity to experience pregnancy and the birth of a child. This loss is both physical and emotional. Physically, they lose the opportunity to feel the growth and development of the child and the accompanying feelings of their own sexual maturity. Emotionally, they lose the closeness that comes from sharing childbirth experiences, including the perceived importance of an early bonding experience with their child.

Finally, infertility threatens the ability to parent. Parenting is a milestone of life: in fact, many people identify childbirth as the single most important event in their lives. Infertility in itself does not deny a man or a woman an opportunity to parent, but the perceived threat is strong. The news of permanent infertility is often devastating.

These losses through infertility have varying degrees of impact on your life and on your partner's life. It is important that you examine these losses and their relative effects. Only then can you make an informed, impassive decision about your future options. If, for example, the loss of a genetic link is important to you but not to your infertile partner, then assisted reproduction may be the option for you to pursue. If joint creation of a child is most important in your lives, failing this, your best option may be to pursue a child-free lifestyle. If, on the other hand, the opportunity to parent is clearly the most important issue, adoption may be the best choice for you.

Few people have the emotional resources to make family-building decisions while struggling with the uncertainty of infertility. Nor should they. Only when a couple have faced and accepted permanent infertility are they ready to move on to decisions about other options.

2

THE DECISION TO ADOPT

Once you have worked through any infertility issues that may be appropriate to your situation, made some decisions about your ideal life-style, and examined your motives for adoption, you are ready to move on to making a decision about adoption.

There are several adoption-related issues, however, of which you should be aware before making a commitment to adoption as a way to build or expand your family. As much as these are facts about the differences that adoption brings, they are not insurmountable differences. Families built by adoption have many more similarities to than differences from families built biologically, but you need to be aware of the differences.

As a parent of an adopted child, you frequently confront adoption-related issues. You can resolve some issues quite easily. Others you can accept as unanswered questions and lay them to rest. Other issues are more weighty, and for better or worse, you must confront them in a manner appropriate to the age of your children and their ability to understand the issues.

The most obvious difference is that adoption will always be a part of your life and your child's life. Your child will always have two sets of parents, you and his biological parents. He may even remember a life and family members before his adoption.

Your child will most likely wonder about her birthparents and the existence of any biological siblings. Her questions may range from wanting to know where she got all those freckles to why her birthparents were unable to raise her. She may fantasize about what life would have been like had she continued to live with her birthparents.

Physically, your child's appearance may be so dissimilar to yours as to cause him to stand out as an adopted child in your family. This difference is especially difficult for a child who also stands out from his friends, another constant reminder of his adoption.

If you adopt transracially or transculturally, beyond becoming a family built by adoption you also become a transracial or transcultural family. Unfortunately, racial prejudices remain in our society. You must be prepared to experience such prejudices, to prepare your child for them, and to teach her how to adjust to them.

When your child is young, you as the adult encounter the prejudice; when your child is old enough to understand for himself, he will be the victim of the subtle or not so subtle bias. Although residence in a racially and culturally diverse community may expand cultural sensitivity, your child must still be prepared to encounter prejudice outside his circle of friends. For your family, the disappointments of your child's inferior treatment will be compounded. You will be unable to soften the prejudices or completely understand their nuances. The solutions that you offer for coping with the frustrations will often fall short.

For these very reasons, many adoptive parent support groups and adoption professionals advocate strong adoptive parent intervention for their transculturally or transracially adopted children. They suggest that adoptive parents provide cultural links and opportunities for continuing contact with children of similar cultural or racial backgrounds. (As a professional organization, the National Association of Black Social Workers has taken a strong stand against transracial adoption because of the loss of a cultural connectedness that such an adoption can bring.)

In addition, medical and social histories the rest of us take for granted may be missing or incomplete for your adopted child. Children adopted internationally frequently have incomplete records. Records for domestic children may not contain information about the birthfather's medical or social history. In fact, few records are updated to reflect subsequent discoveries after the adoption is completed.

Sometimes, unless you have ready access to your child's birthparents, even the simplest of questions may have to go unanswered; for example your child's genetic tendency toward early or late growth and development.

Many of these issues may seem like minor irritants in a busy adult's life. Consider the issues, though, from the perspective of your adopted child, who may not have the maturity or reasoning ability to understand the issues or weigh the alternatives with which her birthparents struggled.

Consider, first, the simplest of scenarios: Your child, whom you adopted domestically, is a blue-eyed blond. You and your spouse both come from a family of brunettes. When your child is young, it is easy for you to laugh off the continuous "Where'd he get the blond hair?" questions by mentioning other blond children in the family. How will your child react when he is old enough to understand the questions for himself?

What about more obvious physical differences? Will your family and community accept a child whom you adopted transracially? What issues will she face in making friends and building a life? Where will she go to meet other kids who look like her?

What about your child's birthparents? Will your son understand that finances, immaturity, or the responsibilities of other children in the family prevented his birthparents from raising him? What about other families who raise all their children despite the same hardships?

When the prospect of adopting a child is only an idea in your mind, it is sometimes hard to understand the importance of these adoption issues. Since the child is not yet a reality to you, the associated problems may seem at arm's length also. These very issues become strikingly important, though, when you care for and desperately love the child who joins your family through adoption.

Friends and families may try to be sensitive, but unfortunately, negative feelings about adoption are common in society. An offhand comment from a grandparent or an unconscious stare from a coworker serves as a vivid reminder of the differences that adoption means.

Your reaction to these insensitivities, though, provides your child with ideas for her own coping mechanisms. Some situations can be pleasantly corrected. Others can be changed through education, and still others can be ignored. What is important is that (1) you recognize that society, in general, has negative feelings about adoption and that these negative feelings have a way of popping up at the most inappropriate times; (2) an adoption-built family is different from families built biologically; and (3) adoption is a way in which people who love each other can be together and be a family.

There are weighty issues in adoption. Thankfully, though, as a prospective parent of an adopted child, you are not alone. A vast network of support groups exists, and they are made up of families just like yours who wanted to build or expand their families through adoption. Some parents adopted domestically, some internationally. Some adopted healthy infants, others chose waiting children. Some adoptions were transracial or transcultural, others were not.

Whatever the individual differences, a common bond exists in these families. This bond is the love of the children who entered their families through adoption and an intense desire to help the children successfully adapt. Adoption support groups can help prepare you for the special challenges of adoption before your child arrives, and they can help you meet the challenges of parenting an adopted child.

3

SUPPORT SYSTEMS

Support systems are critical to a successful adoption. Basically, there are two types: structured and informal. Both are important.

A structured support system is any one of the numerous adoption-related parent support groups, such as the Adoptive Families of America or the North American Council on Adoptable Children. An informal support group is the friends and family whose values and opinions are important to you.

Adoption Support Groups

An adoptive parent support group can offer you many educational, counseling, and support services, such as the following:

- Information and advice from successful adopters. They can tell you which agents and agencies have successfully placed children in your area. They know who is competent and reputable.
- Opportunity for networking. The people in your adoption support group are adoption advocates to a greater or lesser extent. They probably still have contacts with adoption professionals and, possibly, birthparents who may be considering adoption.
- Suggestions on how to proceed with your adoption. All the adopters in your support group have different stories about how they adopted their children. They know that

each situation is different, and they will help you with ideas for tailoring an adoption to your own circumstances. If you are a single person who would like to adopt a child from Central America, for example, it is likely that contacts from your support group can link you with a successful adopter who has experienced similar challenges.
- Ideas about adoptive parenting issues. Many of the parents in your group will have already experienced the issues you will be facing with your child. They can help you get over the hurdles. They will know the books to recommend, the language to use, and just the right times to discuss adoption with your child.
- Information on community resources. A local support group can save you hours of frustration by providing you with information on community resources. Whether you need nutritional information for a low birth weight child or specialized counseling services, your adoption support group can help connect you to the appropriate community services.
- A peer group for your children. Adoption support groups provide an opportunity for children to get together and meet other kids like themselves. Some groups may even subdivide into smaller groups that focus on specific issues or special interests—Asian children, for example. Even if a specific subgroup does not exist or does not meet your needs, the opportunity to socialize with other adopted children is important for some children who may feel different from their non-adopted friends.
- A kindred spirit. Your parents and friends probably do not understand your stresses of infertility and adoptive parenting. A support group can offer friendships, people with common interests and experiences who can understand your feelings and help you.

In addition, some support groups may offer the following:

- Information on waiting children. The North American Council on Adoptable Children, for example, advocates for waiting children and their permanent placement in adoptive homes. Such groups may offer profiles of waiting children as well as information on adoption and postadoption services for these children.
- Legislative advocacy and research information on adoption and adoption issues.

Major metropolitan areas frequently offer a variety of parent support groups. Some may function as an inclusive group that encourages participation from all families touched by adoption. Others may focus more specifically—on single-parent families, families with Asian children, or families with children with special needs, for example. In addition, some groups may function as information providers, offering seminars based on a variety of adoption-related issues, for instance, and others may be geared more socially, limiting themselves to periodic get-togethers to enable the children to enjoy mutual friendships. Before joining an adoptive parent support group, learn about its goals and services and choose a group that seems most suited to your needs.

Family and Friends

The second support group, your family and friends, are those people whose opinions you value most. You probably share similar upbringing, experiences, and values with the people in this support system. They are the people who often tend to be your barometers when you contemplate major life decisions.

If you are considering adoption, you have probably tested the water with this group. Maybe you casually mentioned, "I'm getting older and it doesn't look like I'm getting married anytime soon. Maybe I'll just skip the husband part and adopt a child." Or "Pete and I think we could be pretty good parents. We've even thought about adopting a child with some special needs."

Your statement may have appeared casual, but your interest in their response was anything but. If they seemed supportive, you may have explained your reasons or even divulged that you had already done a little checking. If the response was negative, you could easily have laughed off your remark and then on your own considered their objections and decided whether to pursue your idea.

The reaction of this friends and family support system must be carefully considered. Is a negative response indicative of the response that you (and your adopted child) will receive from society at large, for example? Or is it based on old-fashioned ideas about who is allowed to adopt or what makes a family?

On the other hand, is a positive reaction indicative of a good decision on your part? Or is it just general support for a friend who always seems to make things happen?

In the final analysis, the decision is yours. The support of your family and friends is important. With time and education, any negative feelings that they have may be altered. If this support system is working against you, though, you must decide for yourself whether the merits of your decision to adopt are substantive and whether you and your child can thrive without such acceptance. If your parents could never, ever accept you as a transracial or a transcultural family, can you and your child live without their acceptance? What if this means severing contact with your family for the sake of your child?

SUPPORT SYSTEMS

Both structured and informal support groups can be important in a successful adoption. Joining an adoptive parent support group can be an important vehicle for obtaining information and cultivating friendships in the adoption community both before and after adoptive placement. The acceptance and support of your friends and family are equally important for you and the child you parent through adoption.

Yes, you can manage without the support of either an adoptive parent group or your family and friends. Adoption is more than being able to manage, however. Adoptive parenting is a unique method of family building complete with its own challenges. Support groups can help you find the child you want and help you parent that child happily and successfully.

Part Two

WHY IS ADOPTING A CHILD SO DIFFICULT?

Two major factors affect the adoption process—the availability of adoptable children and the legal system of controls.

At any one time, hundreds of thousands of singles and couples in the United States are waiting to adopt a child. Despite the customary barriers, which may include high costs, long waits for a finite number of adoptable children, and sometimes confusing legal regulations, these prospective adoptive parents are anxious to build or expand their families through adoption.

Adoptions are taking place across the United States every day, however. There are many children in need of permanency and many birthparents who are unable to parent their children.

Although the adoption process seems at times to be an unmanageable legislative nightmare, efforts are being made to safeguard the rights of all those involved. What seem to some lengthy waits for termination of parental rights, for example, are intended to protect birthparents from hasty decisions made during periods of emotional stress.

Courts and legislatures are trying to make adoption a workable plan that provides permanency for children. Across the nation, each state is charged with the responsibility of

WHY IS ADOPTING A CHILD SO DIFFICULT?

looking out for the welfare of its children. Legislatures are recognizing the needs of children for permanency and, as a result, have tried to streamline the process of child placement.

The societal and legislative forces that have shaped modern adoption influence all adoption plans. A working knowledge serves to help you through the adoption process and successfully adopt the child who best suits your adoption plan.

4

SUPPLY AND DEMAND

In the early part of the twentieth century, when there were more children needing permanent homes than there were families willing to take them in, adoption was a relatively easy method of family building. Changes in society since the 1950s, though, have resulted in the restriction of adoptions among nonrelated people.

Family styles have shown some of the most sweeping changes. The divorces and remarriages that were once kept secret are now routine. Stepfamilies are common, and single-parent households are accepted as functional family units.

Parenting practices have also changed. Pregnant women, wed or unwed, are accepted as contributing members of society, and the number of single women who choose to parent their babies is high. Also, fathers are playing a greater role in the upbringing of their children, both in caretaking activities and in parental rights decisions.

Many of these societal changes can be attributed to the effects of the birth control pill, the legalization of abortion, and the rise in feminism. They have all contributed to reduce the number of adoptable babies (particularly white babies). Although it is true that greater attention is now given to the emotional needs of women who decide to make an adoption plan, the number of women choosing adoption for their babies is low compared with those who wish to adopt.

As the supply of adoptable babies dwindled, the demand remained high by comparison. The 1980s and 1990s have been significant for the large number of infertile couples wanting babies. Many waited until their thirties to become pregnant and then experienced difficulties. For others, the use of contraceptives or the presence of insecticides and pollutants reduced their fertility. For whatever combination of reasons, the number of infertile couples wishing to adopt greatly surpasses the number of adoptable infants.

Despite the lack of adoptable infants, other adoptable children await placement. In the past, these placements were often slowed by antiquated policies. Until recently, agency social workers continued to limit adoptions by not reexamining long-established definitions of what constitutes a suitable match between adoptive parents and children. By not making special needs adoption more easily accessible to various groups of prospective adopters, agencies created a situation that resulted in few adoptive placements for adoptable children awaiting placement.

Thus, modern adoption has been influenced by (1) a huge reduction in the number of white infants in need of permanency and (2) restrictive placement policies for waiting children.

5

ADOPTION LAWS: "BEST INTEREST OF THE CHILD"

A major effect of the lopsided supply-and-demand situation of adoptable children has been increased creativity on the part of prospective adoptive parents. Modern adopters have looked for and found success in adoptions that were previously considered nontraditional. These adoptions were, in many cases, completed outside the rigid controls of agency adoptions.

Many pursued international adoptions to fill the void of infants being placed in the United States. Others adopted privately through attorneys or other adoption agents and avoided the scrutiny of agency workers. Still others, particularly singles and older couples, adopted waiting children: sibling groups, older children, or those who were challenged physically or emotionally.

Prospective adopters continue to find ways of locating adoptable children on their own. They are learning more about the adoption process and adoption issues and examining their ability to parent children with different needs.

Protective Legislation

As the scope of adoption practices broadened, it became more important for the legal system to react with laws protecting children and regulating the adoption process. One significant legal development was the acknowledgment of the rights of children. Another legal and social development was the acknowledgment of the rights of birthparents, especially with regard to making choices about the adoption of their children.

Unfortunately, there is no state-to-state uniformity in adoption laws or their interpretation. Legal interpretations in one state may directly contradict those in another state. These differences are often a source of confusion to the general public.

A huge discrepancy in adoption laws across the country serves further to complicate a process that is neither consistently supervised nor uniformly regulated. Added to this is the societal posture that adoption serve the needs of its clients, the children, rather than those wishing to adopt. When disagreements occur, often the custody rights of both adoptive and birthparents and the rights of the children involved are at issue. Although attempts have been made to employ a uniform adoption law among all the states, no such acceptance has been accomplished at present. The legal issues remain unresolved.

A second source of confusion in the adoption process is identification of the actual client adoption serves, namely the child. Although it may seem as if the clients are at times the birthparents and at times the prospective adoptive parents, the true concern of all adoption advocates is, and must continue to be, the child.

Adoption laws are molded not only to serve the needs of the child but also to reflect the attitudes of society charged with protecting children: thus the wide variety in adoption laws from state to state.

Best Interest of the Child

One guiding principle that unifies adoption laws and judicial decisions concerning them is the principle known as the "best interest of the child." Stated simply, this principle dictates that the child's welfare is a determinant in decisions concerning placement. The best interest of the child is not the only guiding principle in adoption laws and judicial decisions (birthparents' rights are strongly considered also), but it is a safeguard that serves to prevent adoption abuses.

Recent court cases challenging adoptive placements have brought the issue of the best interest of the child to national prominence. In some adoption challenges, the courts have found the child's welfare—bonding with an adoptive parent, for example—to be a strong influence in judicial determination; however, in other cases, the parental rights of birthparents have proven most significant.

Part Three

CHANGES IN ADOPTION PRACTICES

Many and varied changes in the adoption process have occurred in recent years. Most of the changes can be summed up in one word: *choice*. Modern adoptions have resulted in increased options for birthparents and adoptive parents. Birthparents have a choice in who will parent their children. Prospective adoptive parents have a choice in the type of child they would like to adopt, the style of adoption, an adoption professional to help complete the adoption process, and, if they select infant adoption, the birthparents of the child. Both birth and prospective adoptive parents have choices in their degree of involvement in the process itself and in the amount of ongoing contact after the adoption is completed.

All in all, there is good news in current adoption procedures: a wide variety of children await adoption, children of all races, ages, needs, and abilities; both birth and prospective adoptive parents have choices in planning the adoptive situation; and adoption agents and agencies are available to help complete the adoption.

Although there remains a place for traditional confidential adoption, many changes are taking place. Birthmothers are demanding a choice in who their child's adoptive parents will be and are gaining legal opportunities to make these decisions. Social service agencies are recognizing parent-child bonding and encouraging the adoption of children by foster parents. Adoptive parents are more informed, more assertive, and less fearful of the adoption procedure. Adoption agencies are changing to meet the needs of their clients. Most importantly, adopted children are benefiting by prompt, guided placement.

A Place for You

The result is that there is a place for you in a system that seems, on the surface, to be steeped in tradition and bureaucracy. This system, which often denied access to all but the most "ideal" parents, has been forced to come to grips with the changing structure of society and to provide options for both birth and adoptive parents. Many, many options are available to those who wish to adopt.

6

MOVEMENT TOWARD OPENNESS

The picture of adoption in the United States has changed dramatically. There no longer is one *only* or even *best* way to accomplish an adoption. Both adoptive and birthparents are realizing that they have options in adoption. The key to a successful experience for all the parties in the adoption circle—birthparents, adoptive parents, and the child—is to find an adoption plan that benefits everyone.

Birth and prospective adoptive parents now routinely decide on the degree of openness they prefer in an adoption. Those who favor ongoing contact can pursue an open adoption situation. Confidential adoptions, those in which there is no identifying information or contact, are also available. There are many variations that can be tailored to suit the individuals involved in an adoption situation.

Movement Toward Openness Options

The concept of openness in adoption has grown in acceptance over the years. The idea of allowing communication between birth and adoptive parents evolved in the late 1970s from adoption professionals' concern for all three members of the adoption circle: birthparents, adoptive parents, and adoptees. Through a policy of more open communication, the professionals believed, birthparents would be able to find peace of mind in the active role of planning the best future for their child, adopted children would be less likely to feel rejected by their birthparents, and adoptive parents would have an opportunity for a more honest relationship with their child and would feel more comfortable with the knowledge that the birthmother was secure in her decision.

Although the idea of openness in adoption evolved slowly, before long a small number of adoption agencies across the country quietly responded to the changed needs of their clients, making ever so slight adaptations toward increasing the opportunities for communication between birth and adoptive parents. As a result, a number of variations on the idea of open adoption have emerged. Ultimately, changes in adoption policy have ranged from providing adoptive parents with pictures and a written record of the history of the biological family all the way to completely open arrangements in which both families have access to one another over the years.

Publication of the book *Dear Birthmother* by Phylis Speedlin and Kathleen Silber in 1983 helped spotlight the issues behind openness in adoption. The book is a series of letters between birthmothers and adoptive parents. It illustrates the genuine care and concern of birthparents for their children and also the sense of relief that comes from knowledge that the child is receiving the best nurturing environment possible.

Today, openness in adoption continues to be studied and discussed on a daily basis. There are three variations of openness in adoption spread across a wide spectrum: confidential adoption, semiopen adoption, and open adoption.

Confidential adoption involves the adoption of a child between anonymous birthparents and adopters. This process nearly always involves an agent or agency that takes control of the matching decisions. Usually the adopters receive nonidentifying information, such as medical and social histories, about the child, but the two sets of parents enter the agreement presuming that any further contact will cease, at least until the child is an adult.

Semiopen adoption involves the sharing of information (usually nonidentifying) between birth and adoptive parents through an intermediary. Birthparents often select the adopting parents, often by screening résumés provided by an intermediary, and may or may not have a face-to-face meeting and ongoing letter or picture exchange.

Open adoption is defined as the choice made directly by a set of birthparents and a set of prospective adoptive parents to arrange an adoption between them. These adoptions involve full disclosure of identifying information between both parties and can include an agreement to maintain ongoing direct contact for the benefit of the adoptee.

7

EXPANDING OPTIONS

The Expanding Role of Birthparents

Not all birthparents desire ongoing contact with the children they place for adoption, nor do all birthparents favor confidentiality. What these birthparents want is a voice in the future they choose for their children.

Birthparents want the peace of mind that comes from knowing that they made the best available adoption plan for their child. The plan frequently includes choices in adoptive parents, the adoption professional, the degree of initial contact, and the degree of ongoing contact.

Those choices are different for each adoption situation. One birthmother may contact an adoption agency, choose a prospective adopter from a group of parent profiles, and limit future contact to yearly photos until the child turns eighteen. Another may answer an adoption classified advertisement, meet the prospective adoptive parents, hammer out a detailed plan of ongoing contact, and then work with an adoption professional, who completes the process for the adopting parents.

Decisions a birthparent makes with regard to ongoing contact are usually influenced by two determinants: her assessment of her own emotional status and her feelings about the best interests of her child. Those birthparents who decide to end or greatly limit contact after adoptive placement may believe that they (and the adoptee) can best go on with their lives by breaking ties. Those who favor ongoing contact may believe that the benefits of continued access—

genetic connectedness, for example—outweigh the risks of possible confusion over parenting roles or identity issues.

As unnerving as some of these options may appear to prospective adopters, a successful adoption comes from shared goals for the child. If as a prospective adopter you believe that ongoing contact with birthparents is not in the best interests of the child you hope to adopt, then by all means look for an adoption situation that reflects this belief. If, on the other hand, you value the opportunity for ongoing contact, seek an adoptive situation in which the birthparent(s) also favor this arrangement.

New Options for Prospective Parents

Adoption in the United States has changed for prospective adopters almost as dramatically as it has for birthparents.

Prospective adopters are becoming educated in adoption issues. They are learning about the types of adoptable children and different styles of adoption. They are talking with adoption professionals and other adopters. They are shopping for agents and agencies that can help them adopt a child who will fit their family. They are challenging the traditional profiles of good parents and redefining old ideas of what makes a family. They are seeking out community services that will help their adopted children adjust to their new lives. And, in the words of adoption activists, they are becoming shameless advocates for children.

Across the country, thousands of agents and agencies are actively involved in adoptive child placement. Many are specialists who assist with a certain type of adoption. Some agencies exist for the sole purpose of placing domestic infants, for example. Others find homes for waiting children. Still others serve children internationally. Some perform all three functions.

In many states, prospective adoptive parents are becoming actively involved in locating birthparents on their own. They are using adoptive parent support groups and their own networking systems and are mounting successful advertising campaigns to expand their options and locate adoptable children both domestically and internationally. Those who wish to adopt waiting children are accessing photolisting books themselves and demanding information on waiting children.

Many of these prospective adoptive parents are weighing the merits of openness in adoption and, in many cases, meeting the birthparents of the child they wish to adopt. Some choose to maintain a degree of ongoing contact. Others choose to terminate contact, usually until the child reaches adulthood.

In some adoptions, prospective adoptive parents are actively involved in communicating with birthparents on their own. They not only find the birthparents themselves, they may take an active role in sharing the pregnancy experience and planning for the birth of the child along with the birthparents. In other adoptions, the agents or agencies take complete control and contact the prospective adoptive parents only when the child is legally free for adoption.

In all adoptions, costs and waiting times vary tremendously depending on the fees of the individual agent or agency, the services they provide to both birth and adoptive parents, and the birthmother's expenses that the prospective adoptive parents are legally permitted to pay. As a prospective adoptive parent, you are free to compare fees and services and choose the adoption option that best suits your goals for adoption and your own unique family situation.

8

WHO CAN ADOPT?

Until recently, traditional adopters were white, under thirty-five, middle to upper class, two-person couples who had been married over five years and who had experienced permanent infertility. These were the ideal couples identified by adoption agents, who frequently tried to "match" the physical characteristics of the adopting couple with those of an adoptable baby. Sectarian adoption agencies customarily added the requirement of religious belief and involvement in church activities.

Three major changes took place in the latter half of the century, however, to change the definitions of "acceptability" for parents in modern adoptions: (1) additional need for adoptive family placements, specifically an increase in the need for permanent homes for waiting children; (2) an opportunity for prospective parents to be evaluated by birthparents on their own merits rather than against rigid agency standards; and (3) lobbying efforts by adoptive parent groups, who challenged traditionally held definitions of what makes a good parent. The result was a tremendously expanded definition of who can successfully parent a child. Models were taken from the successes of biologically built families headed by singles, by gays and lesbians, by older parents, and by physically challenged parents.

Make no mistake that an adoption is notably easier for you if you neatly fit the traditional adopter's profile. If you are a nontraditional prospective adopter, however, it is still possible, and feasible, for you to adopt. You must be more creative in locating an adoptable child. You probably need to depend more heavily on an adoptive family support group, preferably a group for nontraditional adopters like yourself, for moral support and ideas on how to proceed with your adoption plans.

As a nontraditional parent, you will probably find that raising children presents more challenges to you than to a more traditional family. Single parents, adoptive or biological, encounter challenges that married parents usually find less overwhelming: sharing parenting duties and modeling of opposite sex roles, to name two. Gay or lesbian parents, as well as parents of transracial or transcultural children, face the societal burden of prejudice against both themselves and their children. Parents over forty face the physical difficulties younger parents field with ease.

The really great news, though, is that you are not excluded from adopting a child based only on your differences from a somewhat arbitrary definition of a good parent. It really is possible for you to adopt a child!

Part Four

WHO CAN BE ADOPTED?

The tens of thousands of children who are adopted every year represent a cross section of our global society. Adoptive families are built across racial, cultural, and geographical lines. There are children who joined their adoptive families as infants. Others joined at a much later age, often as a part of a sibling group. Some are physically healthy. Others have multiple handicapping conditions.

For some children, birthparents made a prebirth adoption plan that guided the adoption procedure. Many other children were "in waiting." They may have been international children who awaited an often lengthy bureaucratic procedure of international adoption. They may have been some of the 100,000 children in interim care who were either legally free for adoption or who had adoption as their permanent placement plan.

9

DOMESTIC WHITE INFANTS

Although there are more people wishing to adopt U.S.-born white infants than there are adoptable babies, it is possible for you to adopt a healthy white baby. The majority of domestic white infants are adopted through private agencies or independent adoptions. Most domestic white infants become legally free for adoption because the birthmothers choose to make an adoption plan before or shortly after the birth of the child.

Although it is true that many birthparents choose to raise their children, there are still many who choose to make an adoption plan. Increasingly, these birthparents take an active role in choosing the adoptive parents for their children. Birthparents may seek out an agency or agent, or they may respond to an advertisement posted by you or your adoption agent.

Many agents and agencies exist to help birthparents in choosing adoptive placements for their children. After an initial contact, these adoption professionals provide interested birthparents with written résumés, photographs and story narratives, or videos of prospective adoptive parents. The parties may or may not meet, exchange identifying information, or maintain ongoing contact after the initial selection.

If the birthparents choose to work directly with prospective adoptive parents, after the initial contact the parties may continue to communicate themselves or they may employ the services of an adoption specialist. Some parties choose to involve the adoption professionals early on; others prefer to work out the details of the adoption themselves before enlisting professional services to assist with legal requirements.

If you would like to adopt a healthy white infant, first contact an adoptive parent support group near your home. Members can give you information on agents or agencies who are currently placing domestic white infants.

The adoption professionals can give you estimates of the costs and waiting times involved in such an adoption. These agents generally have a network of sources—college sorority houses, gynecologists, and so on—for locating birthparents who are interested in making an adoption plan. Your agent may make the initial contacts with birthparents, or he or she may guide and assist you in making contact yourself. Fees for domestic infant adoptions may be on an itemized basis to cover expenses and fees or they may be a set sum based on the average cost of an infant adoption.

The requirements for prospective adoptive parents also vary with each adoption agent or agency. Age, marital status, and religious preference may be strictly regulated, particularly in agency adoptions. In discussing your adoption plans, you may be asked to make decisions about such issues as acceptable health or medical problems and the degree of ongoing contact with the birthparents. Since most, but not all, domestic white infant adoptions are planned before the child is born, you will probably have little choice in the sex, physical characteristics, or age of the child at placement. (In many cases, an adoptable infant is placed in interim care until the birthparents relinquish their rights to the child. The length of time to complete this procedure varies from state to state.)

10

INTERNATIONAL CHILDREN

Children from other countries are frequently legally free for adoption by U.S. citizens. Africa, Asia, Central and South America, and Eastern Europe are the countries of origin for most international children adopted in the United States. If you wish to adopt an international child, you must comply with the adoption laws in your own state, U.S. immigration laws, and the laws of the child's birth country.

Infants as well as older children may be adopted internationally. Because procedures may often be lengthy, however, an infant may be a number of months old before being released for adoption in the United States. Most international children, especially those who have been living in orphanages, are basically healthy, although some may have minor, correctable medical problems, such as low birth weight or developmental delays. (For information on adopting international waiting children, see Key 13.)

The laws governing international adoption differ tremendously from country to country and within each state in the United States. The adoption professionals who specialize in international adoptions have contacts in selected countries; they know the regulations and customs and are experienced in working with local officials. Some countries allow parent-initiated adoption; that is, you may identify an adoptable child, obtain a legal adoption decree in the child's country, and use the services of your in-state agent. (See Key 24.) Be aware, however, that very strict regulations govern the definition of children who are eligible to be adopted by U.S. citizens.

An appeal of some international adoptions is that, since each country sets its own regulations about international adoption, the regulations, including laws on who may adopt, vary from country to country and may be more flexible than the regulations of agencies serving domestic children. Some countries may allow adoption by singles or older parents, for example, but some U.S. agencies may discourage such adoptions. A definite advantage to international adoption is that the waiting time for your child can be short, often a year or less, particularly if the child has already been born and is waiting for placement. Also, if the child is already born, you have an opportunity to designate a preference for the sex of the child, a situation that is less common with most domestic independent adoptions, which are generally initiated before the birth of the child.

An unfortunate aspect of some international adoptions is that although many proceed very smoothly, others are caught up in seemingly endless red tape. Fees can vary from a few thousand dollars to tens of thousands depending on the child's nationality and the whims of local authorities. Although some countries allow the children who are being adopted to travel to the United States with an escort, other countries require you to travel to the country to complete the adoption. It is not uncommon in some countries, for example, for you to be required to stay in the country for days, even weeks, while local officials complete adoption documentation.

Parents who have adopted internationally suggest that if you are interested in adopting a child internationally, you should take the following steps:

1. Join a support group before adopting your child. A support group can fill you in on the how-tos of accomplishing your adoption, offer networking opportunities, and provide ongoing assistance in helping your child adjust to living in a different culture.
2. Be flexible. Certainly you will have preferences about the country from which you would like to adopt. You may have cultural ties to the country or an affinity to a certain locale. Allow yourself some options, though, in case adoptions are not being allowed through that country at the time that you choose to adopt.
3. Shop around. Many agents and agencies assist in international adoption. Be picky, and ask a lot of questions. Since much of the adoption process will be conducted long distance and quite possibly in a foreign language, you must make an educated choice of adoption facilitator.

11

CHILDREN OF COLOR

African-American, Hispanic, Native American, and Asian-American infants and children also need adoption. Prospective adoptive parents may contact either an adoption agent or a private or public agency for help in locating an adoptable child. You may also contact an agency specifically oriented toward placing children of color.

The large number of children of color who await adoption has resulted in an extensive outreach program by many adoption agencies to attract same-race prospective adoptive parents. Agents and agencies who specialize in placing children of color often seek to fill the void of same-race adopters through active recruitment and by making the adoption process more friendly.

Many prospective adopters, for example, mistakenly believe that they must have a certain income or own their own homes before they can be eligible to adopt a child. Others choose not to pursue adoption because of the time constraints of traveling to the agency to complete paperwork or because of a belief that the assessment procedure is invasive and insensitive. Others refuse to be a part of a system that exists through an exchange of money for children.

By getting the word out that there are children waiting for placement, by communicating that an ability to love and care for a child is more important than financial assets, by working with prospective adopters in their own communities, and by considering the prospective adoptive parents' sensitivities and time constraints, adoption professionals are making progress in placing children of color with same-race parents.

Although social workers and adoption professionals prefer to place children of color with parents of the same ethnic background, and some states mandate such placement, traditionally there have been more children of color legally free for adoption than there have been same-race couples waiting to adopt. As a result, some of these children may be adopted transracially.

A notable exception to transracial adoption occurs with Native American children. The Indian Child Welfare Act of 1978 has strict dictates about children who are of Native American descent. Definitions vary from tribe to tribe regarding Indian status of a person of mixed race; however, the tribes customarily seek adoptive homes within their members to maintain the Indian heritage and culture of the child.

If you decide to parent a child of color transracially, you must be aware not only of the obvious issues of prejudice toward minorities, but also prejudice against transracial families. In addition, many children of color have special needs that range from skin care concerns to a need for cultural connectedness and pride in their heritage.

12

CHILDREN IN INTERIM CARE

Interim, or foster, care is another avenue to adoption that you may want to consider, particularly for toddlers through school-age children. The children are typically temporary wards of the state who have been removed from the home and placed in protective custody. Although the intent of interim care is to work with parents to remedy the offensive situation and return the child to the home, many interim care children eventually become legally free for adoption.

Many children in interim care suffer the long-term effects of the situations that brought them into protective custody—neglect, abuse, and abandonment—and subsequently have special placement needs in their adoption. Occasionally, there are children in interim care who have been removed from the home who suffer no ill effects from the original environment. Included in this group are children who have never been in the offending home environment but who were placed in interim care because of a previous history of neglect or abuse in the home. In such cases, when the parents have not responded to court-ordered counseling or parent education classes, newborns may be removed from the parents at birth and placed directly in interim care.

The state department of human resources is often successful in finding adoptive homes for both types of children through their own agencies. Some waiting children, however, are referred to private agencies specializing in their placement.

Because of the importance of bonding and because bonding may take place between the child and the interim care parents, interim care parents are frequently granted first opportunity to adopt children who have been in their care and whose permanent placement plans include adoption. This practice permits prospective adoptive parents to serve as interim parents for a child who is likely to be freed for adoption. If and when the child becomes legally free for adoption, the interim parents will have the first opportunity to adopt the child. These situations, in which a child is placed in the temporary custody of a prospective adoptive couple before the child is legally free for adoption, are called legal risk adoptions, or fost/adopt.

As the name implies, there is an element of risk in this type of adoption. Basically, there are two disadvantages to this type of adoption: (1) the adoption process may be very lengthy, and (2) the child may never be freed for adoption and may, in fact, be returned to the birth family. Before pursuing a legal risk adoption, you should be sure that you understand the risks involved.

Despite the risks, this is a viable way of locating an adoptable child. A legal risk adoption offers you an opportunity to get to know the child on a day-to-day basis before you actually make a commitment to adoption. If you have experienced difficulty in formulating a workable adoption plan, this may be an avenue worth pursuing.

Depending on your locale, legal risk adoptions may be a relatively untapped source for adoptable children, and it's possible that you may have difficulty obtaining information about this type of adoption. Your state department of human resources (see Appendix B) can provide you with information on the interim care system in your state and the availability of legal risk adoptions. Also, your local adoptive parent support group may be able to offer information or help connect you with someone who has completed a legal risk adoption.

As with other types of adoption, it's important to arm yourself with correct, up-to-date information before you pursue a legal risk adoption. One of the barriers that you may encounter in this type of adoption is a lack of knowledge on the part of agency staff workers, who may not be aware of such legal risk adoptions in your state.

13

WAITING CHILDREN

The largest single group of adoptable children are waiting, or special needs, children. Although the majority of waiting children placed for adoption are U.S. born, many international waiting children also wait to be adopted.

Special needs children are often called waiting children because they are sometimes a part of the interim care system: legally free for adoption and merely waiting for a permanent home.

In the United States, most of the waiting children have entered the interim care system through court order; that is, as a result of such circumstances as neglect, abuse, or abandonment, the courts decided that placement in interim care was in the best interests of the child.

Waiting U.S. children have many similarities:

- Almost half are children of color.
- Many have attention deficit disorder and learning disabilities.
- Their handicapping conditions tend to be multiple.
- Many are older children, frequently above the age of seven.
- Many are part of sibling groups.
- Many have had multiple placements.
- A vast majority have been physically and sexually abused.
- Many have been raised in group homes as part of the interim care system.

- The majority have had access to education in the public school system.

Waiting international children, on the other hand, have a slightly different profile:

- They are often placed voluntarily by parents who feel incapable of raising them.
- They are frequently raised in orphanages.
- Like U.S. waiting children, they tend to be older children and are frequently part of sibling groups.
- Medical attention is frequently lacking for the many who are malnourished or who have medical problems.
- Most are uneducated.
- They are accustomed to few comforts: they have often adapted to living with emotional upheaval and a simplicity of life.
- They are usually emotionally stable, although they are also frequently very dependent on other children and their caretakers because of fewer opportunities to develop independence.

If you would like to adopt a waiting child, your agency worker can match you with a child and help you obtain counseling and support. Before you adopt a waiting child, though, adoption professionals suggest that you consider the following:

1. What are your own motivations for adopting? Adoption is a lifelong commitment, especially when adopting children with special needs. Many of these children have a history of disappointment and lost relationships. Additional disruptions can be devastating to the child.
2. Consider the types of children who are waiting for adoption and your own preferences for the type of

child you would like to adopt. Many states have a photograph listing book with up-to-date profiles of waiting children. Your agency worker should provide you with additional information on specific children, but remember that you are never obligated to accept a child who is referred to you.
3. What is the role of the adoptive family? As an adoptive parent, one of your services to your adopted child is to help him make sense of his past. Love is not enough and adoption does not fix problems, but acceptance, counseling, and support can help him deal with important issues in his past.
4. Obtain a complete medical, physical, and social history (including anecdotal and school behavior) of any child you may be considering for adoption. You would be wise to obtain a good independent prognosis for the child: don't go only by information or opinions provided by the agency. You should also insist on speaking personally with all foster parents of the child. Don't rely solely upon summaries that have been provided to you.
5. What is the availability of ongoing support services for your family? Before adoptive placement, you need to know about financial assistance in the form of any subsidies that may accompany the child, medical coverage for the child, community-based services, especially in the schools, and parent support groups for help and support from someone who has experienced what you will be facing.

Part Five

STYLES OF ADOPTION

When you first considered adoption as a way to build your family, the most important issue was probably the type of child you could adopt. Next came concerns about costs and waiting times. Certainly these are valid concerns. However, adoptive parents will readily tell you that adoption does not end when you take the child home from the hospital, meet her at the airport, or move a family of four from an interim care facility into your own home. Adoption is a lifelong process and the related decisions that you make have long-term effects on the success of the adoption.

A key decision is the choice of an adoption professional. Not only must you judge a lawyer or an agency on the likelihood of the prompt, appropriate placement of a child in your home, but you must also weigh the costs, related services, and integrity of the professionals involved.

Right now, you also need to be making decisions that will affect the next ten to twenty years of your adopted child's life. Will that child (and your family situation) be best served by access to information about her birth family? How much access is beneficial? How much is too much? How will she feel when she is an adolescent and trying to establish her position in society? How will she feel when she is an adult and thinking about becoming a parent herself?

Finally, you need to be aware of the challenges your child will be facing. As an adopted child, she will be unique based solely on the manner in which she joined your family.

What additional differences will she have? How will you help her cope with these differences?

The style of adoption you pursue is determined by several factors: your choice of an adoption professional, the degree of confidentiality preferred, and the decision to adopt domestically or internationally. The choices you make now will have long-lasting ramifications.

14

AGENCY OR INDEPENDENT?

The terminology used to differentiate between adoption agents and agencies and their related services is often confusing. Adding to the confusion is the variety of state statutes under which agents and agencies must operate.

Basically, each state licenses adoption programs that may operate in that state, and generally, all the agents or agencies in that state must comply with the same regulations and guidelines. The differences are generally in the services provided by individual agents or agencies.

Traditionally, agencies provided care and shelter for unwed mothers and found suitable homes for the infants, or they operated in conjunction with state or private orphanages to find homes for older children. In the first half of this century, when far more children than adoptive homes were available, the agencies were primarily nonprofit organizations operated by the government or religious groups.

With societal changes that included a huge swing in the number of birthmothers choosing to parent over adoption and the acceptance of out-of-wedlock pregnancies, homes for unwed mothers all but disappeared.

As the number of adoptable infants declined, the role of both public and private agencies began to change from finding suitable homes for infants to serving birthmothers in finding suitable adoptive placements for their children. Independent agents, a relatively recent addition to the adoption scene, emerged ready to serve prospective adoptive parents by finding adoptable babies. These prospective adoptive parents were often willing to pay large amounts of money for their services.

As the dust settled, two types of adoptive service providers took over: public organizations that looked for homes for the children who were wards of the state and private organizations and individual agents who placed adoptable babies, usually healthy white infants or international children. (Some private agencies continue to serve children who are wards of the state, usually waiting children.)

In addition to licensing adoption agencies, some states also license adoption agents. These licensed agents may include attorneys specializing in adoption, social workers, and adoption consultants who provide what is termed independent (also called private or nonagency) adoption.

Like agencies, agents may offer a full range of services, such as counseling, parenting classes, or child placement, or they may provide only a single-item service, such as legal representation.

Adoption Agencies

Public social service agencies tend to be similar from state to state: they usually serve primarily waiting children, adoption fees are generally low (often on a sliding scale based on the applicant's income) and are frequently subsidized for the adoption of waiting children, and waiting times for healthy infants are long. These public agencies can usually provide you with all the necessary services to complete an adoption, including initial screening, pre- and postplacement counseling to birth and adoptive parents, parent preparation, and legal representation.

Private adoption agencies, on the other hand, vary in a number of aspects: the types of adoptable children whom they serve, the requirements for adoptive parents, costs, waiting times, and the degree of openness available in individual adoptions. The waiting time for an infant, for example, can vary from a few months to many years. Specific requirements regulating such areas as religious affiliation, age, or marital status of applicants are common in private agencies and vary with each agency. Costs also vary with the services provided and the status of the children involved. Waiting children, such as sibling groups or children with physical limitations, for instance, are often wards of the state, and the fees associated with placement are frequently low or reimbursed by the state department of social services.

Like the public social service agencies, private agencies can also generally provide you with a complete range of adoption-related services.

Adoption Agents

Adoption agents may be attorneys, doctors, or adoption professionals who assist in independent adoptions. Most often attorneys or social workers who specialize in adoption, adoption agents may be any person or group providing adoption-related services. These services may or may not include counseling, conducting parent preparation classes, advertising for birthmothers, screening birthmother leads, assisting the birthmother in obtaining medical assistance, handling the disbursement of funds, providing legal representation, and overseeing adoptive placement.

Also included in this group are lawyers who offer only advisory services, legal assistance, or intermediary services during the adoption process; social workers, who offer parent preparation classes, supervision of placement, counseling services, or court representation; and international adoption agents, who assist with international adoptions. Some agents may assist you in finding and screening birthparents; others may merely provide you with associated services that do not lead to contact with a birthmother or an adoptable child. Currently most states permit independent adoptions through an adoption agent.

15

CONFIDENTIAL, SEMIOPEN, OR OPEN?

For some couples and in some adoptive situations, the option of a completely confidential adoption with no contact between birth and adoptive parents may be the best choice. In a confidential adoption in most states, birthparents who contact an adoption agency have the option of choosing an adoptive couple based on nonidentifying résumés or profiles, or they may choose to have the agency make the selection. Adoptive couples usually receive medical and social records for the child and, frequently, a letter and mementos from the birthparents for the child. When the child is an adult, he may have the option of obtaining his adoption records and contacting his birthparents.

As another option, many believe that a semiopen adoption is the best marriage between openness and confidentiality. The mystique of the unknown is erased when birth and adoptive parents have an opportunity to meet face to face. The adopters have access to the child's birthparents and medical and social information. Also, although there is no continued presence of the birthparents in the life of the adopted child, birthparents and the adult adoptee can meet if and when they desire.

Every adaptation of open adoption is different because of the uniqueness of the people involved, but in a somewhat typical form of a semiopen adoption, a birthmother may choose you based on an advertisement that you wrote or by selecting your profile or video from a number of others furnished by your agency. After the initial selection process, you meet before the birth of the child and then again when the child is born. Continued contact is usually limited to yearly letters and photographs sent through the agency.

At the other end of the spectrum, the concept of complete openness in adoption may elicit fears in some prospective adoptive parents. They may envision a reluctant birthmother seeking continued contact with her child, a contact that both interferes with the bonding between child and adoptive family and serves to confuse the child.

In actuality the situation is usually very different. If a birthmother is carefully screened for her true intent about planning an adoption and if she receives adequate counseling so that she is aware of her choices and the emotional stresses that may follow, she is less likely to have a change of heart or, after placement, to interfere with the child's well-being. Of course, no one can guarantee that a seemingly well-adjusted, stable birthmother will not have a change of heart after placement. This is the risk of this type of adoption.

In a typical open adoption, the birthparents may interview you and make their selection after one or more face-to-face meetings before the birth of the child. This personal, direct communication may include the services of a mediator or counselor but it certainly includes full disclosure of identifying information and an agreement to maintain ongoing contact. After the birth of the child and his or her placement in your home, the birthparents continue to play an ongoing role in the child's life, often visiting at your home. Generally, birthparents do not share parenting roles with you but act instead as interested family friends, much like the role of a close aunt or uncle.

Many parents who have participated in open adoptions relate the positive aspects of the experience both at the time of placement and throughout their ongoing contact with the birthparents. They believe that openness serves to help their children learn about their heritage, understand the reasons behind the choice for adoptive placement, and experience the love and concern of an extended family. Another of the benefits of open adoption is the acceptance of birthmothers and the true difficulty of their decision in choosing adoption.

Making a Choice That's Right for You

Whichever adoption style seems at first thought to be most beneficial to you and your adoptive situation, be aware of the following:

1. Your primary concern must be the welfare of your adopted child and the other children in your family.
2. The success of any of the styles of adoption depends on counseling. The importance of appropriate counseling services cannot be overstated. When both you and the birthparents are fully prepared and informed about the short-term and long-term effects of your decisions, your chances for a successful adoptive placement are greatest.
3. In most cases, adoptions can be made more "open" as time goes by, but openness cannot be reversed. As time passes in the life of your adopted child, her needs will change. You may wish to initiate or expand communication with your child's birthparents. Wise foresight about the value of ongoing communication is difficult to ensure for the benefit of birthparents, adoptive parents, and the child. It is better to leave your options open than to overextend your relationship in the early stages.

16

DOMESTIC OR INTERNATIONAL?

A commonly held misconception is that international adoption is somehow easier than domestic adoption. The truth is that neither type of adoption is particularly easy. Although there are many similarities, there are also major differences between international and domestic adoption.

Both international and domestic adoptions may be accomplished through an agency or agent, depending on the laws in the child's country and the adopter's state. Both must comply with certain regulations (such as a state-approved home study or parent preparation classes). Both are frequently time consuming and expensive.

There are many differences between adopting an international and a domestic child, however:

- International adoptions are often favored by many who have a certain affiliation for a specific country or area of the world.
- Criteria for adoptive parents may be less rigid in some countries than those required by certain U.S. agencies, although the foreign adoption process itself may be more cumbersome.
- Adoptable international children are generally waiting in an orphanage, whereas domestic adoptions most frequently involve newborns or older children in interim care.

- International children may truly be abandoned; their medical and social records are frequently incomplete or missing.

Parenting an international child presents a variety of issues not found in a same-race domestic adoption:

- The child's obvious physical differences not only from the other adoptive family members but also from peers
- Societal prejudice against certain ethnic groups
- Societal expectations based on physical characteristics (for example, "All Asians are good in math")
- The child's feelings about a lack of a sense of a cultural connectedness

Changes in governments and economic conditions result in rapid changes in the number of children legally free for international adoption from any one country. If you are interested in adopting internationally, consult an adoptive parent support group, an adoption professional experienced in adoption in the country of your choice, and an international adoption information source, such as the *Report on Foreign Adoption* (International Concerns Committee for Children; see Appendix A). The information you gain from these sources is only a starting point, however. You must educate yourself not only about the process of international adoption but also about the issues in parenting an international child.

Part Six

THE LEGAL PROCESS OF ADOPTION

The importance of sound legal advice and assistance in adoption cannot be overemphasized. Not only does each state fashion its own laws governing adoption, but these laws are often in a state of flux. Recent proposals and changes in some state laws have opened birth records to adult adoptees, allowed birthparents a choice in the adoptive placement of their child, streamlined the process of clearing a child for adoption, and acknowledged the importance of bonding relationships between a child and his or her psychological parents.

A working knowledge of the adoption laws in your state will get you started in making your own adoption plan, but the legal aspect of adoption is no place for a do-it-yourself approach.

If you are working with an agent or an agency licensed by your state, you can be fairly well assured that state regulations will be followed. (Check with your state department of human resources for a list of licensed agencies or agents.) Interview two or three attorneys, agents, or agencies and select the one whom you believe has a good working knowledge of adoption in your state, who can furnish you with references from others who have adopted, and with whom you can easily and comfortably work.

17

REGULATIONS AND PROCEDURES

Regulations

Generally, individual state adoption laws pertain to five areas: licensing agents and agencies, regulating and monitoring adoption practices and procedures, regulating the screening of adoptive parents, regulating the legal process of terminating parental rights, and establishing custody of minor children.

Most state statutes allow adoptions to be performed by either an agent or a licensed adoption agency. A handful of states, though, specifically deny independent adoption, requiring instead that all adoptions be performed by a licensed adoption agency that screens couples, conducts home studies or parent preparation classes, and follows placement of children.

Each state differs in its regulation of adoption practices and procedures. Some state statutes specifically outlaw or regulate the use of advertising to attract birthmothers; other states allow it. In other states, legislatures have not even addressed (and therefore not prohibited) advertising for birthparents.

Most states strictly monitor the fees and charges paid by adoptive parents, however. In some states judges have discretion in interpreting the regulations, allowing for the acceptance of reasonable costs. Acceptable charges generally include medical costs of the pregnancy, such as prenatal care, delivery, hospital charges, tests, prenatal vitamins, counseling, and legal fees, and may in some jurisdictions also include living expenses. Courts determine each case on the basis of similar or related cases in the community. Agents and agency fees must be reasonable and are subject to court approval, and birthparents are expressly restricted from making a profit from their involvement.

One area in which the states seem to be in agreement is screening of adoptive parents. Prospective adoptive parents must complete a home study or parent preparation class and submit various legal and health records, including birth, marriage, and divorce certificates, state police record checks, and medical statements. One major difference, however, is the timing of the home study. For example, in many states in an independent adoption the home study occurs after placement and is far more perfunctory than a usual preplacement home study.

In some states, parental rights are not terminated until the court enters a final adoption decree. In other states, the court determines that it is proper to terminate the parental rights of the birthparents, at which point the child becomes legally free for adoption. In these states, after the birth of the child, the adoption agency or agent petitions the court for a hearing in which the birthmother formally relinquishes her rights to the child. Generally, the purpose of this hearing is to determine whether the birthmother understands her rights and is voluntarily giving up her rights to the child. Often a waiting period of a few days or weeks follows before the termination of rights is final. During this waiting time the birthparents may petition the court for a reversal. In some states, reversals are not granted unless the birthparent(s) can prove that their parental rights were somehow violated, such as through fraud or misrepresentation; in other states, birthparents may revoke the termination at will. At the end of this period, the child becomes legally free for adoption.

Once you have complied with all the requirements and have been given custody of a child for the purposes of adoption, the courts may continue to monitor the child for up to a year or more by requiring that the licensed agency continue to make home visits on a regular basis. At the completion of the supervision process, you are granted permanent custody and issued a new birth certificate identifying you as the child's parent.

Despite the apparent differences in state laws governing adoption, the goal of each jurisdiction is to protect the child and attempt to ensure a stable environment.

Procedures

Generally, legal action in an adoption is not initiated until after the birth of the child. In some states, once the child is born the adoption agent or agency may petition the court on behalf of the birthparents for an appointment for relinquishment of parental rights. At this hearing, the birthparents must declare their voluntary desire to place the child for adoption. (In some states, a consent form signed by the birthfather may be acceptable to the court.) If the judge believes the decisions to be voluntary, he or she grants termination of parental rights, denying the birthparents any future claim to the child. In other states, the birthparents sign consents to adoption rather than participate in a court termination procedure.

Some courts require that a child be placed in interim, or foster, care until the process of termination of parental rights is completed. If the child has been in interim care until this point, he or she may be placed in an adoptive home for the purposes of adoption.

At this point, the child in the adoptive home is a ward of the state until the adoption is completed, usually after a period of several months to a year, at which time a judge grants the adoption, thus giving the adoptive couple permanent custody of the child.

Some licensed private adoption agencies process the licensing of their prospective adoptive parents to provide interim care of the child in anticipation of an adoptive placement. Despite the inherent risk of bonding between adoptive parent and child before the termination of parental rights, many adoptive and birthparents favor immediate placement in the home. Adoptive parents immediately assume the role of caretakers of the child and have early knowledge of the child's health and habits. Birthparents often favor the plan since it provides a continuous environment and relationships for the child.

18

JURISDICTION, INTERSTATE, AND INTERNATIONAL ADOPTIONS

Jurisdiction

Jurisdiction is the legal term that means the authority or territory empowered to interpret and apply the law. Jurisdiction in adoption is important because in many cases a child is born (or resides) in one jurisdiction and you reside in another. If both parties reside in the same state, jurisdiction usually involves the authority of the courts in the county of residence of each party. If both parties reside in different states or countries, jurisdiction involves the authority of the courts in both states or countries.

In a single-state adoption, jurisdiction is a relatively minor issue since the same laws govern the adoption process. Jurisdictional questions generally concern only the location of the individual court where legal proceedings will take place.

If you are dealing with an interstate adoption, it is necessary to check the jurisdictional requirements of both states. Interstate adoptions must comply with regulations in both the sending and receiving states and with the Interstate Compact on the Placement of Children.

International adoptions must also comply with U.S. immigration laws. Depending upon whether the countries involved are signatories to the Hague Convention on Inter-Country Adoption, you may also have to comply with the terms of this treaty.

Interstate Adoption

For any number of reasons, you may consider interstate adoption. If you know of a potential birthmother in another state, for example, or of an adoption agent or agency that has been extremely successful, you may want to consider interstate adoption. Generally, though, adoptions are always easier when both you and the birthparents reside in the same state.

All states participate in the Interstate Compact on the Placement of Children, which governs interstate adoptions. If you plan to adopt a child from another state, your agent must know and comply with the requirements prescribed by the Interstate Compact on the Placement of Children. All interstate adoptions must be approved by the interstate compact administrators in both states, and you are not allowed to transport the child across state lines until you obtain both approvals.

Because of the need to comply with laws in two jurisdictions and the constraints of distance, interstate adoptions can be more expensive than in-state adoptions. Regulations are very exact, and failure to comply can void your adoption. You should make sure that you have knowledgeable legal representation. A mistake by an attorney inexperienced in interstate adoption can cause frustration and delay.

Many adopters have been successful in interstate adoption, however. If you have been experiencing difficulty locating an adoptable child in your own state, you may want to consider expanding your search.

International Adoptions

Depending on the laws of their own state, applicants for international adoption can use the services of an agency in their own state or they may combine local and out-of-state services. In many states, for example, they may use local services for parent preparation classes and an out-of-state agency for locating an adoptable child, dealing with foreign officials, and conducting other foreign procedures.

Increasingly, prospective adoptive parents are pursuing parent-initiated independent adoptions to find international children. Attorneys who specialize in these placements are knowledgeable about the adoptable children in various countries and each country's placement regulations. As with interstate adoptions, if you wish to adopt internationally you must also comply with the laws of the receiving state.

Regardless of the method you choose, it is imperative that you work with reputable contacts. All international adoptions must meet three criteria: (1) they must comply with the laws of the state where the adoptive parents reside, (2) they must comply with the laws of the child's birth country, and (3) they must comply with U.S. immigration laws.

Support groups, such as the Adoptive Families of America, can provide you with the names of area parent groups who have built families through international adoption and the names of agencies that work with international adoptions.

19

SAFEGUARDS FOR A SUCCESSFUL ADOPTION

Illegal or unethical adoption practices are difficult to hide given the strict regulations and regular monitoring practices in most states today. Certainly such cases, although they exist, are much less common than attention-grabbing headlines and scare tactics lead us to believe.

The majority of situations that make headlines usually fall into one of two categories: misrepresentation on the part of the adoption agent or agency or a change of heart by a birthmother.

Regularly, stories of unscrupulous adoption attorneys or social workers receive media attention: for example, prospective adoptive couples who wait years and invest thousands of dollars only to discover later that the baby they were promised never really existed. Other real-life cases of adoptions gone bad involved agencies that failed to disclose adopted children's preplacement mental, physical, or emotional condition to their adoptive parents.

Those isolated cases of fraud frighten us all and cast a shadow over all adoption. Although it seems as if common sense is a sufficient safeguard against many of these incidents, these and other unfortunate, and perhaps not deliberate, situations in adoption do occur.

Cases of birthparents changing th[e]
ing to parent their children, for exam[ple]
associated with many adoptions. The[y]
as dramatic as the headlines lead
especially compared with the great n[umber of]
adoptions. This is not to negate the intense fe[el]
pointment and despair a birthmother's change of he[art]
bring to an adoption plan. In addition, a birthparent's change
of heart can also result in the loss of large sums of money
the prospective adoptive couple invested in prenatal expenses. Most states allow an adoptive parent to pay for certain pregnancy-related costs, such as medical bills and, in some states, food and housing. A birthmother who changes her mind is sometimes required to make reimbursement for these expenses; however, collection is often difficult. Insurance is available, in some instances, to recoup the costs when a birthmother changes her mind.

Although no one can predict, much less ensure, the success of any particular adoption before the process is completed, there are steps that you can take to improve your chances for completing an adoption successfully.

The best safeguard to decrease your risk of an unsuccessful adoption is to have up-to-date information, professional advice, and common sense. As always, if an adoption situation sounds too good to be true, it probably is. Not only do you want your efforts to result in the adoption of a child, you also undoubtedly want the experience to be as positive as possible for all parties involved.

Here are some actions you can take to minimize the chances of disappointment:

1. Know your state laws, and work with your own attorney or adoption agency. An adoptive parent support

group can inform you about state regulations and guide you toward professionals who have helped others successfully adopt in your state.

2. Choose an experienced, reputable agency or agent who will represent your best interests. Not only should your agent be experienced in the type of adoption you would like to pursue, he should be a person who will present himself well to birthparents considering adoption. He needs to be accessible, likable, and trustworthy. Above all, ask for and check references of parents who have adopted through the agent or agency you are considering. It's important also to check the agent or agency with your state adoption specialist, the Better Business Bureau, the state licensing entity, and/or the state attorney general.

3. Obtain a written estimate of the adoption professional's exact services and fees as well as any additional fees or payments for which you will be responsible. Make sure you also have a written agreement detailing the procedure to be followed in the event that an adoption is not completed. The agent may be unsuccessful in helping you adopt a suitable child, or you may, for whatever reason, decide not to complete the adoption plan. Make sure you understand your options. Do not be intimidated into avoiding these issues. An experienced adoption professional should routinely answer these questions and readily provide you with this information.

4. Do not exchange money with a birthparent (or her representative) without the advice of your attorney or agency. States often regulate payment of prenatal expenses by adoptive parents, and thus payment of nonapproved expenses may be in violation of state law and may jeopardize your adoption. Also, many

pregnant women qualify for economic assistance that covers prenatal expenses. Assess your individual situation. If the expenses seem too great for you to shoulder, look for another birthmother.
5. If you are too apprehensive about the potential for financial fraud or a birthparent's change of heart, work with an agency that shoulders the financial responsibility up front and passes the costs to the adoptive couple after the adoption is completed.
6. If you sense that influential family members or friends are opposed to the birthparents' decision for adoption, you may want to find another situation. (This is an example of the advisability of prenatal counseling for birthmothers. Some changes of heart are difficult to foresee, but a professional counselor may be able to spot a woman who is wavering in her decision to place the child.)
7. Obtain as much information as possible about the child and birthparents, including social and medical histories and the circumstances related to the decision for placement. (This is critical if you are adopting a waiting child.) Your intermediary may be helpful in obtaining some of this information.
8. If you are considering a special needs child, you need to obtain an independent diagnosis and prognosis of the child's condition and then realistically assess your ability to parent the child. If you are considering adopting a sibling group, for example, one child may exhibit more unacceptable behaviors than the other children. Make sure that you can parent this child as well as the other children in the group.

The Importance of Counseling

Time and again, counseling has proven to be a key element in the long-term success of any adoption. This is true whether you are adopting an infant, a waiting child, or an international child. Adoption does not stop when the judge pounds the gavel and declares the child a member of your family. Adoption spans the lifetime of all parties involved and, at various times in this lifetime, counseling may be critically important. A successful adoption does not last a year: it lasts a lifetime.

Unfortunately, adoption is built on loss. Whether it is the birthmother's loss of dreams for the future, an adoptive parent's loss of a genetic legacy, or an adopted child's loss of control or self-esteem, adoption means loss for everyone.

When birthparents are involved in the adoption process, both birth and prospective adoptive parents must understand that the decisions they are making not only affect the welfare of the child but profoundly affect their own lives as well.

Counseling can help birthparents examine their options, accept their circumstances, and make a plan that benefits the child. Before completing adoption plans, birthparents must understand the ramifications of their pregnancies and, if they choose adoption, the stages of the grieving process they will experience. They must also understand their legal rights and options in adoption. Counseling has the advantage of cementing the birthparents' confidence in their choice for adoption.

Undoubtedly, birthparents feel intense grief when they make an adoption plan. Bonding with the child may start when the woman knows she is pregnant, and breaking this bond is painful. Often a birthmother must cope with the emotional loss of the baby's birthfather, who may no longer be interested in continuing the relationship. Another hardship is the birthmother's loss of dreams of a new life and the start of a new family. Finally, the birthmother must often fight the societal pressures of her peers and family, who may consider adoption an act of irresponsibility.

Children who are older when they are adopted, including infants and toddlers who have spent time in interim care, also suffer losses. For some it may be the pains of separation from a caretaker. Others may feel divided loyalties between the parents who cared for them (no matter how inadequately) and the new parents they are supposed to love. Still others may suffer from feelings of rejection or confusion over abuse issues.

As a prospective adoptive parent, you must address your own feelings about infertility and about adoption as well as understand the pain of separation the birthparents and your adopted child experience. Counseling also offers you the opportunity for preplacement parent preparation and discussion of the legal issues and financial aspects of adoption.

After placement and finalization, the need for counseling may still exist. Even though your child's birthparents may be secure in their decision for adoption, they may need to express their sorrow for the loss of their child and seek reinforcement for their decision. As your child grows, especially if she looks different from other family members, she may need help understanding and accepting the circumstances of her adoption. You may need assistance through the course of day-to-day child rearing in addition to coping with the special issues in adoption.

Despite the inevitable frustrations and potential for disappointments associated with modern adoption, it really is possible for you to have a successful, positive adoption experience. By educating yourself, making wise choices, and seeking professional assistance, you can greatly increase your chances for finding the child you want to adopt.

Know the Laws of Your State

The more you know about the adoption laws in your state, the more comfortably you can work within the system. Since every adoption must be approved through the state court system, it is to your advantage to know the rules even before you get started. When you know the rules, you are better prepared to assess individual situations and plan alternative strategies that result in your adopting the child you want. You know, for example, that if you cannot find an agency that can help you, you still have options. Depending on the state laws, you can either proceed through an independent agent or locate a birthmother on your own and work with an agency to complete state requirements, such as parent preparation and legal proceedings.

Knowledge of the laws can spare you not only inconvenience but also the loss of a child as a result of technicalities. An interstate adoption can be voided for noncompliance with the Interstate Compact on the Placement of Children, for example. Your knowledge can also help arm you against unscrupulous dealings you may encounter when trying to fashion your own adoption.

Part Seven

PLANNING AN ADOPTION STRATEGY

Despite current publicity to the contrary, successfully adopting the child of your choice can be accomplished. Of course, if you are willing to wait five to seven years or to spend tens of thousands of dollars to obtain a child, your adoption procedure should be considerably easier. If you have time or financial limitations, however, the adoption procedure can become quite challenging, even disappointing and discouraging, unless you have a plan of action to get you started and sustain you when the going gets rough.

20

A SIX-STEP PLAN

Whether your goal is to adopt an international infant, a waiting child, or a healthy newborn, you need a game plan to keep you organized and moving in the right direction. If your head is not spinning from all the information you have had to take in and all the choices you have made so far, you are lucky. Once you actually dive in and start pursuing a child—making your own adoption happen—you will be relieved to have the preliminary decisions behind you so you can move forward toward implementation.

Here, in brief, is a strategy aimed at helping you accomplish a successful adoption.

First, *make a definite decision about the type of child you would like to adopt.*

There are almost limitless possibilities for types of adoptable children. Such factors as preferences about age, race, special needs, sex, and social and medical histories all have the potential of influencing a person's decision about an ideal child he or she would like to adopt.

The type of child you would like to adopt determines the process you follow in locating such a child. The method of locating a waiting child, for example, is very different from the method of locating a domestic infant or an international toddler. The pursuit of any particular type of child changes with each child based on the variables just mentioned.

Your first step is to make some preliminary decisions about the type of child you would like to adopt. Only then can you chart your course and pursue a plan of action. Otherwise, your attempts are aimless excursions, like a trip without a destination.

Second, *investigate both the state laws governing adoption and the adoption programs currently being offered by agents and agencies both within and outside your state.*

Consult your state's department of social services and your local chapter of an adoptive parent support group, such as the Adoptive Families of America. You will find out about the legal issues pertaining to adoption in your state and the methods and contacts that have proven successful for other adoptive parents.

Third, *assess the amount of money, time, and risk you are willing to devote to accomplish the adoption.*

Think about all the interrelated issues in adoption—degrees of openness, availability of children, timetables, and choices of adoption professionals—and try to formulate a clear picture of how you envision yourself successfully adopting a child. Will you be more comfortable, for example, initiating the adoption of an international child through an adoption attorney? Would you prefer a domestic child to have the opportunity for greater access to the child's birthparents? Can you accept the uncertainty of contacting a birthmother yourself and together formulating a workable adoption plan?

Obviously, there are many factors and options in modern adoption that you must evaluate in terms of your own unique circumstances and preferences. The options vary in relative cost, length of completion time, and risk factors. Probably there is someone in a parent support group who has adopted using a method similar to what you envision and who is willing to share his or her experiences with you.

Fourth, *make a plan of action.*

A support group can help you plan your approach. Many local chapters have regularly scheduled meetings devoted to preplacement issues, such as examining adoption options or locating birthmothers. Through either a formal presentation or an informal chat over coffee, you hear first-hand accounts of methods that have been successful: which attorneys have an active client list, which newspapers have been agreeable to publishing ads for birthmothers, which countries allow singles to adopt, which adoption professionals work with same-sex couples, and so on.

You will have to sift through the mounds of information you receive, sorting and choosing the pieces that will help you accomplish your own adoption. Before long you realize that your own individual plan is taking shape based on your perception of the child you want, your set of circumstances and constraints, and the decisions you are making.

Fifth, *formulate a contingency plan to use if your original plan, for whatever reason, becomes unworkable.*

Adoption plans are not immune to Murphy's law. No matter how well planned your strategy, if something can go wrong it will. There will be plenty of times when you feel like the person in the grocery store checkout lane who waits while every other customer in the store seems to be sprinting through the other checkout lanes.

The knowledge that you have a well-crafted contingency plan will provide you with the emotional support you need when you feel tempted to abandon your plans. Maybe you will choose to employ your contingency plan. Maybe you will decide to make a minor adjustment or to give your original plan more time, but at least you will not feel powerless thinking that you made the wrong choice and you are stuck with it. This is like the sinking feeling when you realize that someone really did close down the cash register and you are still standing in line.

Finally, *put your plans into action.*

You can probably see that the decisions you are making now and the steps you are starting to take are, in effect, limiting rather than expanding your options. This is the way it should be. If you have not already, you could easily become mired in adoption options. There comes a point when you must make some decisions and get on with your plans. Now is the time.

Read through the next keys and begin to put together your own ideas for how you will go about adopting your child. The better you prepare yourself, the clearer picture you will have of how you will actually accomplish your task, including foreseeing problems and preparing contingencies, and the greater your chances for success.

Activating Your Decisions

Regardless of your final choices for your adoption plan, remember that if you want to accomplish a speedy adoption your work has just begun. To be successful, you must do two things: take an active, aggressive role in finding a child, and continue to exercise your options in finding alternative ways to find the child you want.

21

CHOOSING AN ADOPTION PROFESSIONAL

You are now at the point at which you must proceed with your adoption plan. One important decision you must make concerns the adoption professional to assist you.

The states have varied regulations about adoption and the agents or agencies licensed to place children in the home. A handful of states prohibit independent adoption, in which case you must work through a licensed agency. Other states prohibit intermediaries, or consultants, from placing children. In most states, however, you may choose to use either an adoption agent or an agency.

State adoption laws are set up to protect the welfare and best interests of the children. The strict controls, however, also help protect you from situations that may be unlawful, unethical, or just plain uncomfortable. Your choice of an agent or agency to help you depends on the laws in your state, the type of child you want, your own personal restrictions about fees, waiting times, and degrees of confidentiality, and your own sense of comfort with one type of agency or another.

Making a Choice

Start by contacting the agents or agencies that handle the type of adoptions that you prefer and set up an appointment for an initial interview. This meeting gives [a] detailed look at their services. If there is a fee [for] consultation, you must weigh the merits of c[onsultation against the] value of the information. Remember that although [adoption] is intended to serve the best interests of the child, you as a consumer must have answers to certain basic questions about adoptable children, fees, waiting times, and procedures. Before you leave the meeting, and certainly before you put down any money, make sure you have a clear understanding of what you can expect:

- What procedures does the agency make use of, for example, for matching prospective parents with waiting children or with birthmothers?
- How does the agency locate adoptable children?

Any ambiguities left unanswered will be compounded during the stresses of waiting for a child.

Common Services of Agents and Agencies

1. Provide pre- and postplacement counseling, education, and support:
   - Assist adoptive parents
   - Assist birthparents
   - Assist children

2. Find birthparents:
   - Assist in résumé writing
   - Provide mailing lists, contacts
   - Outreach (advertising) for birthmothers

3. Screen birthparents:
   - Address sensitive issues, such as prenatal care and drug and alcohol use
   - Arrange meetings of birth and adoptive parents

4. Find adoptable children:
   - Provide a listbook on waiting children
   - Locate international children

5. Serve as intermediary:
   - Address health issues: birth defects, circumcision, and others
   - Transport an international child
   - Handle the disbursement of funds
   - Forward correspondence between birth and adoptive parents
   - Arrange meetings with waiting children
   - Obtain medical, social, and behavioral information about waiting children
   - Communicate with officials in foreign countries

6. Arrange placement:
   - Receive child when discharged from hospital
   - Monitor placement in home pending completion of adoption

7. Provide services for legal issues and procedures:
   - Screen adoptive parents
   - Explain the legal process
   - Conduct parent preparation classes
   - File the adoption petition

The states also require that you meet certain criteria before placement is made. Some regulation is in the form of providing basic documentation. Another requirement is for completion of a certified home study or parent preparation class. As a prospective adoptive parent, you can expect to provide the agency with the following:

1. Legal documentation (all certified copies):
   - Birth certificate
   - Marriage certificate
   - Divorce record(s)
   - Death certificate of deceased former spouse
   - Birth certificate of other children

2. Medical information:
   - Statement about health
   - Statement about infertility (if applicable)
   - Psychological profile

3. Financial information:
   - Notarized financial statements
   - Verification of employment

4. Personal data:
   - Brief autobiography
   - Photographs
   - References

Increasing Your Chances for Success

Whether you eventually choose to work with an adoption agency, an attorney specializing in adoption, or an adoption agent, adherence to certain safeguards can help ensure that your adoption is successful.

One is an opportunity for ongoing counseling services for the birthparents. When the birthparents are made fully aware of their legal options, have an opportunity to discuss their feelings with a professional counselor, and have an opportunity to examine potential placement options, they are better able to make a rational decision about the child and his or her future.

A second safeguard is the availability of experienced legal assistance. Some adoption agents, workers in understaffed agencies, and attorneys inexperienced in adoption may not have the legal expertise necessary to conduct an adoption. The result can be frustrating delays. Make sure that the people you are working with are knowledgeable about the adoption laws in your state. If you are pursuing an interstate adoption, legal experience and expertise are even more critical. You may even need attorneys in both states or in both countries if you are adopting internationally.

22

STAYING ACTIVELY INVOLVED

If you have not already thought about the next best thing to your first choice of adoption plan, try to start formulating some ideas. There are no guarantees in adoption. Despite your best efforts, you may never end up with the exact child you want. To guard against the utter discouragement such a disappointment would bring, it is important to have an alternative choice—and an alternative game plan—ready to put into effect.

The Value of a Contingency Plan

The purpose of this contingency plan is to function as a safety net. You may never need it, but it is reassuring just knowing it is there. Your contingency plan helps you operate from a position of strength, not one of weakness, and positively affects the way you deal with agents, birthmothers, and your own support group. Also, if you make your alternative plan now while you are relatively stress free, it is more likely to be a valid decision, not an abrupt reaction to events beyond your control.

Consider Your Alternatives

Why not pursue a different type of contingency plan? There are a number of alternatives. One is to have another choice of the type of child you would like. If your preference is a domestic infant, why not consider an international infant as an alternative? Another option is a different choice of agency or agent. If you think you would prefer to work with an agency, consider an independent agent adoption as an alternative.

While you think about your contingency plan, think about time. When, for example, will you decide that enough is enough and it is time to put the contingency plan into effect? Your answer can be either a specific date or a specific amount of money—after you have spent a predetermined amount of money on advertising for adoption, for example.

You improve your chances for success by choosing a contingency plan that is rather different from your preferred plan. Do not switch wildly from one agency with a five year wait to another, similar agency with an equally long waiting list because you heard about someone who recently adopted a child through that source.

Keep Tabs on Your Progress

As you have seen, the course of many adoptions is guided by active involvement by the prospective adoptive parents. In the past when would-be adopters enrolled with an agency, they patiently waited their turn until an appropriate adoptable child became legally free for adoption.

Chances are good that you do not have this luxury. Unless you already have access to an adoptable child, you must stay active in keeping your own adoption plan on course. This does not mean daily phone calls to an attorney who is trying to locate an adoptable child, but it means staying in contact, doing occasional prodding, and, if necessary, doing footwork on your own.

Here is a situation that, unfortunately, is not uncommon:

Alan is interested in finding a waiting child to adopt. He has heard that there are thousands of waiting children in need of a permanent home. As a single man and a high school teacher, Alan believes he could successfully parent an older child with some behavioral problems or learning difficulties. After contacting his county social service department and discussing his interest in adopting a waiting child, Alan receives the usual battery of counseling sessions, psychological tests, and parent preparation classes. Alan is told that he has been approved and that he will be contacted when a child becomes legally free for adoption. Four months go by and still no child for Alan.

Confused and frustrated by the lengthy process, he patiently awaits word from his social worker.

Alan's adoption plan may continue drifting along in just such a manner. Shortages of agency personnel may keep Alan—and a suitable child—from meeting until Alan's case makes its way to the top of his social worker's pile.

Alan's mistake was in not learning about the adoption system ahead of time. Most states have an adoption exchange system for waiting children. The state itself may publish a photolisting book of children in need of adoption as well as work with agencies in other states. The National Adoption Center, many agencies specializing in waiting children, and adoptive parent support groups also routinely publish information about waiting children.

Alan needed to arm himself with specific information about adopting waiting children and to make some waves about his desire to adopt such a child.

23

RISKS AND STRESSES

No one will tell you that any adoption is either risk or stress free. Modern adoption is full of both. There are ways to handle and reduce each, though.

The single most important safeguard is the appropriate choice of a placement agent or agency. Your agent can screen potential birthmothers or waiting children and advise you of the chances of that particular adoption being successful. She can also serve as an intermediary between you and any prospective birthmothers, so you want to find a professional who is both knowledgeable about adoption and compassionate about the needs of birthparents. Since counseling is such an important factor, you also want counseling services either through your agent or through a professional counselor.

Like realtors who are employed to work on behalf of the seller, adoption agencies are empowered to work on behalf of the child and the birthparents. In actuality, though, both realtors and adoption agents must also serve all the parties involved. A private adoption agency, adoption agent, or consultant needs to serve you also. She needs to take a personal interest in finding an appropriate child for you. By doing this, she is not working against her stated clients, the child and birthparents, but rather for them by finding the most suitable placement.

A caring, professional adoption agent will make sure that you understand the legal, financial, and procedural aspects of the adoption system in your state. She should explain what she can and cannot do for you in finding adoptable children.

One important role of your agent is to shield you from certain potentialities in an adoption situation:

1. The birthmother changes her mind. Many times this situation is unforeseeable; however, if a professional has reason to believe that the birthmother is wavering in her decision after the birth of the child, the child should be placed in interim care rather than in your home.
2. Demands from the birthmother are unacceptable to you. The agent should act as a mediator and either help you reach an agreement or suggest that another matching be made.
3. It is not uncommon for a birthmother who has chosen adoption or an adoptive parent to experience resistance from hospital staff. The hospital staff may have negative feelings about adoption, or they may be merely unsure about how to deal with the situation. An adoption agent can serve as a buffer between adoptive parties and the hospital staff.
4. You should be counseled to expect negative attitudes of society about adoption issues and also provided with complete information about how to respond when family members or friends ask about the adoption.
5. You can allay your inability to make definite plans for the arrival of a child by becoming more active in locating a birthmother, learning about the child's birth country, preparing a nursery, and so on.
6. The adoption process is hard work and emotionally draining for adoptive parents. A counselor should prepare you for the work involved since adoption requires a strong support system.

Part Eight

LOCATING A BIRTHMOTHER ON YOUR OWN

Many prospective adoptive parents, especially nontraditional adopters, are attracted to the adoption strategy of locating a birthmother on their own. After an initial contact, you may enlist the aid of a professional or make your own adoption plans before enlisting the assistance of an adoption agent or agency to complete the legal requirements. A strong appeal for such a plan is that you are judged by the birthmother on your own merits, rather than against agency standards or alongside more traditional parents in an agency book of profiles. State laws vary about the practice of advertising for birthparents, however, so it's important to know the laws of the states in which you plan to advertise.

These parent-initiated adoptions (which incidentally can be initiated by either birthparents or prospective adoptive parents) are a popular way to locate an adoptable child. Although the method is more commonly used with domestic adoptions, parents who have pursued parent-initiated adoptions have been successful in adopting international children as well.

When you start talking with others who have successfully adopted by locating a birthmother on their own, the process seems remarkably easy. The now happy parents advertised in some way to let others know that they were interested in adopting a child, and they spent some anxious moments worrying about whether an adoption would actually take place—they may have even followed some blind leads and met with a series of disappointments—but now they have a child.

Each adoptive parent's story is different, and yet all these people have successfully adopted. Your situation will be different, too. Maybe you are older than many traditional adopters, or single, or already have a child. You can still listen to the strategies that resulted in a successful adoption for others, make adaptations specific to your situation, and find the child you want.

There are a number of methods of advertising your desire to adopt. Some couples have been successful with mass mailings of thousands of résumés to gynecologists, college sorority houses, lawyers, and so forth. Others get results through word of mouth: that is, by telling every person they know that they are interested in adoption. Still others believe in the power of the press and place newspaper ads in small town or large city newspapers across the country. Each of these methods has worked.

Regardless of the advertising vehicle, you must focus on personalization of your message. Birthparents want to feel that their child will receive lots of attention and will be raised in a manner similar to what they, the birthparents, would provide if they had felt able to parent the child.

24

PARENT-INITIATED ADOPTION

Parent-initiated or self-directed adoption has become a popular alternative for prospective adoptive parents who would like to have greater control over the adoption process. This increased involvement frequently includes the prospective adoptive parents actively recruiting and selecting potential birthparents.

Parent-initiated adoption is basically an adoption designed according to the wishes of both you, the prospective adopter, and the birthparents. Either party can initiate contact, usually through a form of advertising. Together you, and often your representatives, discuss and arrange plans for the adoption. Adoption professionals then implement your plans according to the wishes of the adoptive parties.

Self-directed adoptions were originally a form of independent adoption. Once birth and adoptive parents found each other, they contacted an adoption professional who assisted with the adoption. A slight adaptation of this procedure is followed in states that ban independent adoptions. Agencies serve the adoptive parties in the completion of the adoption according to state regulations. This practice is commonly referred to as *identified* adoption.

For some adoptive parents and many birthparents, the appeal of parent-initiated adoption is the opportunity to be active in your own adoption plan. You may advertise for adoption (in states that do not prohibit the practice). Birthparents may respond to those ads or even advertise for adoptive parents themselves. Although these adoptions may involve the use of professionals for a variety of services—mediation, education, counseling, financial advice, or legal guidance—both you and the birthparents are the key decision makers.

The nature of self-directed adoption implies a measure of contact between you and the birthparents. Since you openly advertise for birthparents, most but not all self-directed adoptions are some form of open or semiopen adoption. You and the birthparents may meet and plan the adoption together, using an agency or agent to complete a home study or other requirements necessary for legalization.

Or, after an initial nonidentifying contact, you may choose to turn communications over to adoption intermediaries and continue anonymous contact through the intermediaries. The agent or agency may speak with both parties separately to arrange an adoption agreeable to both of you that adheres to state laws. Any postplacement communication between you can continue through the adoption professional.

Parent-initiated adoption frequently avoids the major obstacle in most agency- or agent-assisted adoptions: time. When you locate birthparents on your own, you are ready to bypass agency waiting lists and proceed with the formalities of adoption.

Another plus is that self-directed adoption allows you to be selected and evaluated by birthparents on your own merits.

Unfortunately, there are also risks to parent-initiated adoption. You might advertise for months and not receive a favorable response that leads to adoption. In the meantime, you could easily spend hundreds, even thousands, of dollars.

Another very weighty risk of parent-initiated adoption is the possibility that birthparents can, and many do, change their minds, even after you have paid prenatal and birth expenses, and decide to parent the child rather than continue with the adoption plan. This potential for a change of heart is a very real possibility that you must understand and be ready to accept. The emotional loss of a child and of all the dreams that accompany this loss often outweigh any accompanying financial loss. Although exact figures for the percentage of birthparents who change their minds and decide to parent are unavailable, you must be aware of the very real possibility of such an occurrence.

Unfortunately, a small number of women who express an interest in adoption are actually deceptive and never intend to go through with an adoption plan. Sometimes these frauds succeed in working their way through the adoption process because the situations are never fully investigated and the individuals are good at deception.

Despite the risks, many adoptive parents have been successful in locating and adopting domestic or international children through parent-initiated adoption. If you are willing to accept the risks of parent-initiated adoption, agreeable to advertising for birthparents, and ready to implement some marketing techniques, you can greatly improve your chances of finding a child.

Parent-initiated adoption is not for everyone. In many ways it is a very risky way to obtain a child, but when you are successful, the risks do not seem so overwhelming.

The greatest risk prospective adoptive parents face is the potential for disappointment that accompanies a birthmother's change of heart. As a safeguard, work only through legitimate adoption agents and take care to find just the right birthmother. Finding a birthmother who is well along in her pregnancy, who has previously given birth, or who has exhibited definite indicators of a sincere intent is a good start. It is much more reassuring to deal with someone who has already given birth or someone who actually has plans to go on and do something with herself after the birth of the child.

25

ADVERTISING FOR BIRTHPARENTS

Advertising for birthparents has become a highly competitive, very sophisticated process in the 1990s. The current situation of high demand for the relatively small supply of birthparents choosing adoption has resulted in many prospective adoptive parents developing creative and extensive advertising schemes.

Marketing: The Buzzword of the 1990s

The intense competition for children is forcing prospective adopters to shift gears quickly. Most prospective adopters are not far into the adoption process before they find themselves spending their resources thinking of ways to attract birthparents successfully. No sooner do they abandon conversations about infertility grieving than they begin discussing marketing strategies about target populations and mass mailings.

One thing is certain: whether you choose to advertise in the industrial North or the religious South, in a small town or a big city, your ad will compete with the ads of all the other hopeful adoptive parents.

Competition for birthparents has fueled the rise of professional adoption consultants to aid prospective adopters in their search for birthparents. Other hopeful adoptive parents fashion their own marketing plans. Regardless of the avenues you choose to pursue, you have a good chance of being successful in attracting birthparents who want to choose adoption.

A Typical Birthmother

For your advertising campaign to be successful, it must reach and appeal to a birthmother. This sounds simple, doesn't it? Before you start your campaign, however, take a look at a typical birthmother.

First, she is probably insecure and unsure about her decision to make an adoption plan. She may or may not have the support of the baby's father or her own family. She may, in fact, be bucking their express preferences, or they may not know of her decision—or her pregnancy, for that matter.

Second, she wants to feel that she is making the best choice for her child. She wants to feel comfortable that her child will be loved and cared for.

Third, she wants her child to live in a stable environment that is not unlike one that she would provide if she could. This may mean a two-parent family or it may mean greater economic stability. Chances are, she wants a family environment that is not vastly dissimilar from her own.

Fourth, she may want to have an active role in choosing who will adopt her baby. She may ask for some degree of communication and an opportunity to meet the child when he or she is an adult.

As you can see, a birthmother truly may be the girl next door who has had weighty issues thrust upon her. When you appeal to her to entrust the life of her baby to you, try to understand the situation from her perspective.

Where to Find Birthmothers

As with other successful advertising campaigns, targeting your intended audience is a key factor. Adoptive parents have been successful in finding birthparents from across the country or across the street. No one can predict where you will find your child's birthparents.

Nonetheless, there are strong feelings about increasing your chances of success through regional advertising (remember that some states prohibit advertising for birthparents) and target populations. However, this advice does not mean that you must spend thousands of dollars on a national advertising campaign, but it does mean that you should be aware of target populations and fashion your strategies with them in mind.

Some adoptive parents have been successful appealing to birthparents in the South, where religious feelings against abortion are strong. Others focus on the industrial North, where unemployment is high and weak economic conditions can make parenting a hardship.

Birthparents do not always come from select states, highly religious sects, or underemployed populations, though. They come from affluent, middle-class, and poor neighborhoods in the North and South. Many are college students or professionals who are unable to parent effectively at this stage in their lives. Birthparents are in crowded cities and sparsely settled rural areas and everywhere in between.

Certainly there are trends, and you may be concerned with aiming your marketing dollars in the right direction, but in truth, birthparents who make adoption plans come from all walks of life and live in all sections of the country. Chances are good that you have examples of all these conditions in your state.

In-state adoptions, generally considered less costly than interstate adoptions, also have the appeal of easier accessibility between birth and adoptive parents. This is especially important in open adoptions, in which ongoing contact between the adoptive parties is desired.

No population studies can guarantee a source of adoptable children. The studies are useful as indicators, however, and, when teamed with a variety of other factors, can provide usable information that may result in improved chances for success. As with other considerations in effecting a successful parent-initiated adoption, the key is to educate yourself about the influential factors, match the information with your personalized adoption goals, and formulate your own strategy.

Setting up to Advertise

Once you are ready to start actively looking for a birthmother, there are all sorts of avenues you will need to pursue simultaneously. One method will work for you, and this is all it will take to find one baby. The downside is that you do not know ahead of time precisely which method will be successful.

To begin, you may want to consider adding a separate phone line or a multiring service to your existing phone line for the duration of the advertising campaign. Many couples make this an unlisted baby line used solely for this purpose. A separate line and number ensure your privacy and can be removed after you have adopted. Check with the local telephone company about the cost and availability of both options. You may also consider an answering machine for when you are away from the phone. If you plan to install an extra line, make your arrangements with the phone company right away because it may take them awhile to start your service. In the meantime, read ahead and start planning your own advertising campaign.

You want to decide how much money you can spend on advertising and where to concentrate your efforts. Set a reasonable limit to spend in the first three months; at the end of this time you will have a good idea of what advertising methods were effective and should be continued and which should be omitted.

One major decision that you must make is whether to advertise out of state. This has implications for your entire adoption plan since out-of-state adoptions will probably complicate your adoption proceedings and escalate the expenses. You may need to engage an attorney in both states, for example, or you may be required to travel to and establish short-term residency in the birthmother's state or pay to have her travel to your state for the birth of the child.

Whether you decide to advertise in-state or out of state, or both, your adoptive parent support group and your attorney or agent should be able to give you up-to-date information about locales that have been good sources for birthparents who wish to make adoption plans. Since not only state laws but also societal attitudes and economic conditions are subject to change, sources that are consistently active in adoption will prove most beneficial to you.

Also, not all newspapers accept classified advertising for the purposes of adoption. Check with your adoption professional, support group, or the individual newspapers.

Four Popular Methods of Advertising for Birthparents

Four types of advertising methods have proven successful for prospective adoptive parents seeking to attract birthparents interested in making an adoption plan for their children: networking, flyers, mass mailings, and classifieds.

The methods vary in many ways, yet each has proven to be a successful marketing tool. Some of the advertising methods are free; others are moderately to extremely expensive. Some show quick results; others may take long periods of time to prove effective. Some require lots of thought and planning; others can be accomplished in casual conversation. Some are very public, others more private. Based on your own adoption plan, you may choose to employ one or more of these advertising techniques.

Successful advertisers know that repeat advertising is one of the secrets of success: the more you advertise, the more likely you are to accomplish your goals. Other considerations, of course, are your budgetary and time constraints and the degree of disclosure you are willing to provide. Certainly you want your advertising money and energies to be well directed. Take time to look at your advertising options, to consider your own adoption plan, and to target your population so that your energies are directed most efficiently. A well-planned advertising approach provides your greatest likelihood of success.

26

NETWORKING

The easiest and least expensive way to advertise your desire to adopt is by *networking*—communicating your intent to a circle of friends and acquaintances and asking them to spread the word. Tell everyone you know that you want to adopt a child and that you wish to accomplish this by locating a birthmother yourself. Solicit their support in mentioning you to any birthparents they know who may be considering adoption. Stress your openness to communicate about adoption options and your willingness to talk and provide information.

If you have not already done so, join your local adoptive parent support group and attend their meetings. These adoptive parents know the ins and outs of adoption from firsthand experience. They also have continuing contact with others interested in adoption, possibly even birthparents.

Next, approach the usual people who come to mind—your family, friends, minister, physician, and attorney. Then expand your circle. Force yourself to bring babies and your own desire to adopt into conversations. Word of mouth is often considered the best type of advertising. The more people who know that you would like to adopt a baby, the better chance you have of actually meeting someone who wants to make an adoption plan. Networking is a common method of finding a birthmother; a "friend of a friend" system for locating a woman who is pregnant and unable to parent and who wishes to find a good home for her baby.

Some prospective adoptive parents carry informal business cards to give to new acquaintances. The cards include first names, a phone number, and a short message, such as "We'd like to adopt. Please call us collect if we can help you."

Be prepared to find that many people, including your family and friends, react from their preconceived notion that what you are doing is either illegal or immoral and that at best you are headed for disappointment. Your goal is to adopt a child, however, and you need to get the word out that you are looking for a baby to adopt. Do not let these people stand in your way.

27

FLYERS

Another quick, inexpensive way to advertise your desire to adopt is to thumbtack flyers on bulletin boards in high-traffic business establishments. This is a low-key appeal to young adults who may frequent such spots. The flyers can actually be any size of sheets, from index cards to full-page sheets with tear-off phone numbers at the bottom. The purpose is to convey very informally your desire to adopt a child.

As with other types of advertising, try to be unique. Use colored sheets so your message stands out among all the others. Keep your message short, warm, and friendly. You are striving for an at-a-glance appeal to the person who may be scanning the bulletin board in passing. You can mention a little about yourself and your interests, but do not get too personal or too specific. Since anyone is apt to read your message, do not list your name. Include only your phone number or your agent's name and number, inviting birthparents to call collect.

A sample flyer might read: "Adoption: If you are looking for a happy, stable home for your child, please call us. We are a married couple who would like to love your child and provide a good home. Please call us collect at XXX-XXXX or our adoption agent at XXX-XXXX."

The expense of this form of advertising is minimal—the price of 100 flyers, thumbtacks, and gas money and the time it takes to write, duplicate, and deliver the messages.

Although you could have the flyers printed professionally, the method is so adaptive to instant changes that you may decide you prefer to have the opportunity to reword and try again rather than incur the printing expense.

Plan your target areas to obtain the best exposure to birthparents who may be considering adoption. Think about regions in your immediate area, state, or country that are likely to have a relatively high incidence of birthparents seeking adoption for their children. Also consider areas with large populations of women of child-bearing age, such as college campuses. Once you have decided on your target region, consider the type of business establishment in which to post the flyers. Grocery stores, discount or variety stores, theaters or skating rinks, laundromats, dormitories, and health food stores are all worth pursuing.

To sample a variety of locales, try dividing your flyers among out-of-town friends to distribute. Post one set of flyers at nearby businesses. Send another set to a friend in a small town or rural area, another to a friend at a college campus, and the remainder to a friend in a large city. Once you start getting responses, you can ask the callers where they saw your flyer and, if necessary, pepper that area with more flyers.

If your flyers are drawing interest but dead-end responses, try rewording them. Try, for example, focusing more on benefits to the child or a unique talent or hobby you enjoy. The costs in time and money for this type of advertising are so minimal that you can experiment a great deal without much expenditure.

The disadvantages to flyers are twofold. One, your advertising reaches only a relatively small audience. Each flyer may reach only a modest number of readers, an even smaller segment of whom are pregnant and looking for adoption options. Second, the flyers are accessible to a diverse population ranging from idly curious information seekers to members of fringe groups vocally opposed to your method of attracting birthmothers. In other words, you may have to field a variety of unproductive calls, possibly even nuisance calls, in response to your posted flyers.

28

MAILINGS

Some adoptive parents have been successful through mass mailings of single-page résumés. Prospective adoptive parents often blanket an area with these résumés, sending them to obstetricians, crisis pregnancy centers, and college sorority houses or health centers requesting that the résumé be made available to birthparents considering adoption.

A one-page résumé like this can be effective if you can keep it upbeat and conversational. Include key points that would be important to the birthparents and reflective of your personality and what you can offer the child. Your intended audience is a young woman who is probably more interested in you personally than in your life accomplishments.

Various formats can be employed. Some adoptive parents have been successful with letters to birthparents, others with personal narratives, and still others with traditional résumé styles. Choose a style with which you are comfortable, but be sure to maintain a warm, empathetic tone that emphasizes the love and attention you will give to the child.

Your résumé should include brief references to pertinent details in your life, such as other children in your family, career, reasons for infertility, hobbies, life-style, and so forth. A small photograph of yourself that conveys friendliness and that will reproduce clearly is a nice, eye-catching addition. You can feel relatively safe including your first names on the sheet since the audience is more select than those who see an advertisement available to the general public. Be sure to include your or your adoption agent's phone number and a request to call collect.

Along with your résumé, enclose a cover letter to the health center managers, obstetricians, or housemothers who receive your résumé. The cover letter should introduce you, mention your desire to adopt, and solicit the recipient's help. Include relevant information that will legitimatize your request or prompt them to recommend your profile over another.

If you are working with an agent or agency that offers counseling services for birthparents, for example, mention this service since health care professionals who receive your résumé are likely to value counseling in adoption situations. Request that your résumé be made accessible to birthparents considering adoption and that it be posted if possible. Individual policies vary about posting such résumés, but it is important that your message be passed to the right parties.

Mass mailings of hundreds, even thousands, of résumés provide the best chance for success. Adoption attorneys or agents may be able to provide rental lists for wide mailings, or you can obtain local addresses from your telephone directory. If you are attempting to target a market on your own, send your résumé to locales that may have large populations of birthparents likely to consider adoption.

Mass mailings have the potential of being moderately to very expensive. A rental fee for a mailing list adds to the expense of this method of advertising; however, such a list may have a proven track record of adoption successes and therefore be more cost effective than blind mailings. Other out-of-pocket expenses consist of the postage and duplicating or printing charges.

Additionally, you must budget time to plan and design the résumé and cover letter and to prepare them for mailing. The merge function on your computer allows you to personalize your cover letter as well as address the packets.

One of the risks of mass mailings is that your message may never get into the hands of those with whom you want to communicate—birthparents who are thinking about adoption. If you are working with a consultant or attorney who has had good results with mass mailings, however, he or she can advise you about the success rate other clients have had with this type of advertising.

The advantage of résumés as an advertising method is the possibility of preliminary screening. Your résumé is seen by a more select audience, many of whom are birthparents considering adoption. Many of them have direct access to health care professionals who can answer adoption-related questions. Calls are likely to come from potential birthparents who have preliminary information about adoption, who have reviewed your résumé, and who are interested in initiating a conversation with you about adoption.

29

CLASSIFIED ADVERTISING

Classified advertising in newspapers and "advertisers" has proven to be an extremely effective method of attracting birthparents interested in planning an adoption. Adoption ads commonly appear in five types of newspapers: national dailies, large city dailies, medium to small city dailies, local weeklies, and local advertising "shoppers."

Regardless of the type of newspaper you choose, two things are certain: (1) you have a very good chance of attracting a birthmother through classified ads, and (2) if you choose to use classifieds, you must get serious. Classifieds have withstood the test of time. Many successful adoptions have been completed based on an initial appeal through classified advertising. Hit-and-miss advertising is a waste of money, though. More than with any other method of advertising, to be successful with classifieds you must make a definite commitment to your advertising strategy.

Large circulation or small, newspaper classified ads are the big leagues of adoption advertising. Per inch, they are the costliest type of advertising commonly employed by prospective adoptive parents seeking birthparents. Unless you are very lucky, you will not achieve instantaneous success. Ultimate success comes only from repeat advertising.

If you are working with an adoption attorney or agent who has been successful in helping prospective adoptive couples attract birthparents through classified advertising, he or she can give you advice based on experience. Otherwise, with some thought and preparation, you can plan a successful strategy on your own.

Before you initiate a classified advertising campaign, you must have a game plan that includes decisions about where you advertise, how frequently, and for what duration. Even after you carefully fashion and place your ad, though, it is unrealistic to think that your work is done and that success will come to you. You want to continue to analyze your results and adapt your ad if necessary. Reanalysis does not mean completely abandoning your plan and starting over, though. It may mean making slight changes in wording, size, or placement, or it may mean giving your ad some extra time to be effective.

By doing a little research before you begin, you can decide where your advertising dollars are best spent. Carefully consider costs versus circulation. You may be further ahead, for example, spending more money on a national publication, knowing that your ad will reach a much larger audience.

Some papers have regulations banning adoption ads (and some states prohibit adoption advertising). If you encounter a paper with such a policy, just eliminate this paper from your list of choices and move on to one of your other choices.

While you are investigating your classified options, do not overlook the value of advertising shoppers. Usually free to readers, these weekly shoppers are tremendously popular with both rural and urban readers. Although some shoppers include news or feature stories, the majority of the pages are filled with classified and display ads. You may find advertising rates very affordable.

The chamber of commerce in the area you have targeted may be able to provide the name and phone number of the local newspaper or advertising shopper. Also, a number of papers or shoppers may be owned by a single corporation; one phone call can provide access to all their publications as well as special rates. Three bits of advice:

1. Do not be put off by the size of the publication. From the national dailies to the weekly shoppers, each type of paper has its merits. Choose the one that seems right for you and your personal adoption plan.
2. Place your ad right alongside the competition. You have a better chance of being successful if your intended reader knows where to find you. Like any consumer, a birthparent is more likely to look where she knows she has choices. If your ad appeals to birthparents, you have every chance of being successful regardless of the competition.
3. Repeat advertising is critical. A birthparent who is worried about her ability to parent may consider adoption when she first sees your ad. On that initial thought, though, she is probably unlikely to clip your ad, much less call you to discuss adoption. Repeat reminders may jog her memory. When it comes time for her actually to take action, your ad, if it is still handy, may be the one that she chooses. If your ad is not there, she probably will not search through back issues for it; she may even assume that you have already been successful in locating a birthmother.

As with all advertising campaigns, it is important to mark your calendar for a reevaluation date when you will examine your responses and options. At this reevaluation session you may decide to go ahead with another round of advertising, to sit out the holiday season, or even to employ your contingency plan. If you design a reevaluation date into your campaign from the beginning, you will be ready to make advertising a profitable experience. By expecting to reevaluate, you free yourself of the process-stopping reaction that may result from disappointment over your previous results.

Classified advertising has the important advantages of expediency and a proven track record, but there are three major disadvantages: cost, reduced cost effectiveness, and lack of privacy compared with other types of advertising.

1. **Cost:** Newspaper advertising can be expensive to start and to maintain.
2. **Reduced cost effectiveness:** When you pay for your classified ad, you pay for the publication to be distributed to all readers regardless of their value to you as potential birthparents who may be considering adoption. Newspaper advertising allows you to target a locale but not a narrow population.
3. **Lack of privacy:** Since classified adoption ads are very public, you have no control of who calls you. You may be subject to any number of inappropriate calls, from curiosity seekers, to insincere or fraudulent birthparents seeking to extort pregnancy expenses, to activists opposed to advertising for birthparents, to idle prison inmates. These calls can be especially disconcerting if you are already stressed from the anxieties of adoption.

Patterning Your Classified Ad

Before you invest hundreds of dollars in classified ads, take a few minutes to evaluate sample ads from a birthparent's point of view. Primarily, you want to judge whether the ads appeal to a birthparent who is unable to parent and who wishes to make an adoption plan for her child.

Find adoption ads in the personals section of a few sample newspapers. Pick out a few ads you think would be effective. Then try to evaluate why, specifically, these particular ads would be more effective than other adoption ads. (If you do not trust your own decisions, solicit the advice of some young adult friends.) Next, begin to examine the characteristics of the ads you chose:

1. What feelings do they convey: warmth, security, economic stability?
2. How, specifically, do they accomplish this feeling: through descriptive words and phrases, or through references to the prospective adoptive parents, the child, and the birthparents?
3. Are the ads long or short? Are they similar to or different from the other adoption ads?

There are no right or wrong answers, and no one has determined what works and what does not work in using newspaper advertising to attract birthparents. What is important, though, is that you start thinking about classified ads and the subtle differences that wording conveys.

The results of your own evaluation of adoption classifieds may help you in fashioning an ad that, in only a few words, conveys an accurate picture of you and the life that you could provide to a child. You pattern your own ad by selecting bits and pieces from appealing ads and adding your own personal touch.

Ten Tips for a Successful Ad

1. *Treat the reader with respect.* Develop a mental attitude and vocabulary that treats birthparents respectfully. Talk about choices, not problems.

   "Adoption: Are you worried about your unborn child's future?" is a short sentence that gets to the point yet addresses the birthparent's prime concern of a happy, safe future for her child. The question is respectful, almost parent to parent, and implies that the reader is responsible and worthy of respect. The question also suggests the author's mutual concern and implies that a solution is at hand.

2. *Sell benefits, not features.* A birthparent is looking for someone whom she can trust to care for her child. A sensitive ad can communicate this feeling about you.

   A birthmother probably does not care that your spouse has a doctorate. What she cares about is your warmth and compassion. You must tell her by examples, however, not by definition. Tell her that your home is full of books and stuffed animals, not that you and your spouse are warm and understanding.

   For example, "We have a place in our home—and in our hearts—to sit by the fire and read to a child on snowy evenings" may appeal to a wish for her child to have a cozy home.

3. *Appeal to her desire to match her heritage or upbringing with yours.* Word your ad to reflect your family's personality, whether it is love of the theater or love of sports. She is looking for a family whose goals resemble her own for the child. "Family gatherings at the cottage are a yearly event" may remind her of her own childhood and opportunities that she would like her child to experience as well.

4. *Set her mind at ease about you.* She may be distrustful of strangers or of authority figures. Be friendly, and try to convey acceptance of her situation. If you

are interested in open adoption, for example, let her know. She may feel more comfortable knowing that you are agreeable to working with her ideas.

"We'd like to talk with you about open adoption" is a pleasant invitation to call you and discuss adoption.

5. *Guide her in your direction.* The birthmother may be unsure of herself and uncommitted about her plans for her baby. She may feel uncomfortable about talking to an adult, and her friends may not be able to give her any ideas on how to find suitable parents for her child.

   Often, your ad is the point that not only guides her decision but guides it in your direction. You just may be the solution to her problems. Suggest that she call you collect to talk about making an adoption plan. "Please call us collect if we can help you, XXX-XXX-XXXX."

6. *Carefully consider distance.* Remember that a birthmother wants to feel a kinship with you. She may, for example, feel more comfortable answering an ad within her state, especially if she is interested in an open adoption plan. She also may want some amount of distance, however, to preclude chance meetings. Consider mentioning your state, or your telephone area code may be sufficient indication of your general location.

7. *Place your ad where she will see it.* If it is important to you to attract a college student, advertise in a campus town or a national paper. If an East Coast birthparent fits your plans more appropriately, advertise in one of the large eastern dailies. If you have no preference, *USA Today* has been a popular

spot for adoption ads. Of course, many people are likely to pick up and read their own local newspaper or advertising shopper.

8. *Time your ad.* The birthmother whom you want to attract probably really is the girl next door. She is probably going to try to make it through the holiday season without making a decision about her pregnancy. Generally, plan your ad campaigns to avoid holidays and vacation periods, especially if you are advertising to attract a college student.

9. *Save some requirements for a personal conversation.* Even if you really do not want a birthmother who smokes or drinks, do not say this in your ad. Wait until you have the opportunity to talk to the birthmother, or better yet, let your attorney or agent address sensitive issues, such as health or personal habits, with the birthmother.

10. *Do not make her read choppy phrases or wade through abbreviations.* Spend the extra money to talk to her in sentences. "Wntd: Infant to adopt. Can offer lvg, secure home. All exp. pd. Call col. XXX-XXX-XXXX" is really a rather abrupt way to communicate with someone who, you hope, will entrust her child to you.

30

ADVERTISING SUCCESSES AND FAILURES

With so many adoptive parents experiencing success through adoption ads, it is interesting to examine the reasons behind the success of this particular medium. Why, for instance, would a birthmother respond to such a seemingly impersonal appeal for her child? Why would she not choose, instead, to tell her doctor about her desire to make an adoption plan and choose adoptive parents based on a reliable, professional recommendation?

Adoption ads help birthparents over the first and primary hurdle of an adoption decision: considering the option without making a commitment to anyone. A birthmother can glance at an adoption classified without even telling anyone that she is pregnant and considering adoption. All the pertinent information is right there in her living room, yet it leaves no telltale evidence of her interest nor requires a commitment from her. A secondary appeal lies in the sense of personalization that two-party communication conveys. It seems odd to think that a classified ad sounds personal, but the attraction comes from the opportunity for the two parties to talk together without an intermediary.

The success of adoption advertising for birthmothers, particularly classified advertising, indicates that once a birthmother moves past the inquiry stage and decides to pursue making an adoption plan, she still frequently chooses to respond to a classified ad.

Without scientific studies to explain the rationale for this choice, an analysis of the reasons behind the appeal of classifieds is only speculation. It may be beneficial to look more closely at classified advertising to try to uncover the attributes that contribute to its success.

Obviously, a host of personal factors may be influential to any one individual birthparent when choosing adoption. Although other methods of advertising for birthparents have many of the same or similar characteristics as classifieds, subtle differences may account for the undisputable success many adoptive parents have found through classified advertising.

Classified ads offer certain identifiable characteristics that may contribute to their success rate.

1. *They imply an element of physical and emotional distance between the advertiser and the reader.* Physical as well as emotional distance between birthparents and the child and the adoptive family may hold strong appeal to birthparents. Increased distance has a greater chance of precluding chance meeting, and it also offers the romantic appeal of the unknown. Think about how we tend to favor the advice from the "expert" from fifty miles away rather than the opinion of an equally qualified neighbor we have known for years. Birthparents may feel the same way.
2. *Placing a classified ad indicates a degree of demonstrated effort on the part of the advertiser.* Birthparents may also be attracted by the effort prospective adoptive parents must expend to advertise in the newspaper. This effort indicates more

decisive action than what might be considered an offhand remark to a physician. A person who is committed enough to compose and place a classified may appear to have serious intents.

3. *Classified adoption ads make a direct appeal from advertiser to reader.* Through an adoption ad, prospective adoptive parents try to speak directly to a birthparent who is considering adoption. Birthparents can feel a kinship with someone who may be the solution to their worries without third-party intervention.

4. *They offer anonymity to the reader.* A birthparent considering adoption can read an adoption classified in private. She can even respond anonymously. Through this medium the birthparent retains control of the situation, revealing and committing to only as much as she wants at any time.

5. *Each ad is often one of many, similar ads and, therefore, its placement implies tacit social acceptability as well as offering choices to the reader.* A single adoption ad may seem peculiar, but there is legitimacy in numbers. The sheer number of adoption ads is a very subtle, implicit indication of societal acceptance of the method of advertising for birthparents.

Also, multiple ads offer multiple choices. A flyer advertises only one choice of adoptive parents. A doctor or friend can recommend only a handful of interested couples at best, but a classified is one of many choices. Classifieds are the place to look if someone is shopping.

As successful as classified advertising has been, other avenues should not be overlooked. No one can accurately predict which leads will materialize into an adoptable baby. Other methods of advertising, especially those that are easy and inexpensive, are also worth pursuing.

31

INITIAL COMMUNICATIONS WITH BIRTHPARENTS

If you have not already done so, the next step is connecting with an agent or agency to fulfill your state requirements for adoption. When a potential birthmother calls, you will need to have the name and number of your agent or agency to give to her.

While You Are Waiting for the Phone to Ring

While you are waiting for the phone to ring, try some role-playing activities with your parenting partner. It will be hard enough when you get your first call: Neither you nor the caller is experienced in this endeavor, and it will be up to you to keep the conversation going. Here are some ideas that may prove helpful:

- On a tablet by your phone, keep the name and phone number of the agency and individual to whom you will be referring a prospective birthmother.
- Write "have compassion" on your notepad. A birthmother who calls is making one of the hardest decisions she will ever have to make in her life. You can help her by showing genuine concern for her and her situation. Try to keep from focusing on the baby and what the birthmother can do for you. Ask, instead, about her and her interests.

- In this initial conversation you mainly discuss her goals for adoption and attempt to get to know each other a little bit. You may be more informed about current adoption practices than she is. If this is the case, you may want to tell her a little about state laws on adoption, about the agent with whom you are working, and about your own family background and interests. It is OK to talk about prenatal care and insurance, but try to phrase your questions to show that you care about her, not that you are grilling her. If you do not feel comfortable asking a particular question—about insurance, for example—wait for another conversation or ask your agent to address the question.
- At the end of the call, ask for her name and phone number and ask her to contact your intermediary or facilitator.

You may want to make a decision about who fields the initial calls. Even if the male is a better conversationalist, the female may be the better choice. An insecure birthmother may feel more comfortable talking to another woman. She may have difficulty talking to men, the man with whom she was involved may evoke negative thoughts—who knows?

Here are some questions that are perfectly acceptable for the first conversation:

1. Age?
2. Due date?
3. Is adoption a firm decision?
4. What prompted you to make an adoption plan?
5. Have you been seeing a doctor?
6. Do you have insurance coverage for the pregnancy?
7. Is the father actively involved in the adoption plan?
8. Is he willing to sign relinquishment papers?
9. How does your family feel about your decision?
10. Can you tell me a little about yourself and your family?

11. Are you working? How long do you plan to continue working?

Here are some questions that you should be prepared to answer on the first call:
1. What is your occupation?
2. What is your family like?
3. Are there other children in the family?
4. Why do you want to adopt?
5. Do you live in the city or country?
6. What do you enjoy as hobbies and during your free time?
7. Describe yourselves.

What to Do When the Phone Rings

Sooner than you think, the phone will actually ring. Unfortunately, all the calls you get are not from legitimate birthmothers. You can generally expect calls from pregnant women who are seeking information about adoption, pregnant women who are legitimately seeking placement, friends or relatives who think the pregnant woman should make an adoption plan, curious would-be adoptive couples who want to know about your success rate with your advertising, and prank callers.

When the phone rings, try to remember some of the role-playing conversations you practiced. Chances are good that the caller is very tentative. She may even be calling secretly and be forced to hang up quickly. Do not expect her to lead the conversation. If you are stuck for something to say, tell her that you are new at looking for a baby but maybe she would like to know a little more about your family. Again, focus on the benefits to her, not your personal features. Tell her, for example, how kind your husband is, not that he is an award-winning scientist. If you have a huge family that gets together at the lake every summer, mention this. Try to emit warmth.

If you are interested in one of the forms of open adoption, you should explain open adoption options and procedures to her since she may not be aware of the state adoption laws or her rights as a birthparent. She may not know, for example, that she can see the baby in the hospital or even name the child.

Some birthparents, especially if they themselves have been through the foster care system, feel strongly against their baby spending time in interim care until the mother's rights are terminated. If your agency has arranged to have you licensed as an interim care provider so that you can take the baby home from the hospital, tell her this.

In all your dealings, you must be honest and sincere. Some of the callers, however, will not be telling you the truth for whatever reason, and unless you are very intuitive, you do not realize this until later, when you find out they have given you a phony telephone number or have not made the follow-up call to the agency they promised to make.

If you have experienced a number of such disappointments, it is sometimes difficult to keep from being callous when you answer the phone. Unfortunately, this type of disappointment goes with the territory of the public process of advertising for birthparents.

Although it is often impossible to predict who will complete an adoption plan, there are some indicators that may be helpful. Women who end up parenting their babies, for example, are more likely either to have a strong emotional attachment to the fetus or to have a strong ongoing relationship with the baby's father. Conversely, a number of studies suggest that the chances for a successful adoption are greater if the birthmother (1) has terminated the relationship with the baby's father, (2) has the emotional support of a significant person in her life, especially her mother, and (3) has clear and definite goals for her future. (See Key 32 for a profile of a typical birthmother who makes an adoption placement.) At other times, forces that are completely unknown enter the picture and influence an adoption plan.

At any rate, try to keep your conversation light and compassionate. If all your questions are not answered, this is OK. There will be time later. Make sure, though, that you get at least the caller's first name and her phone number and that you ask her to call your agent or agency the next day. You can give her your first name so she can refer to you when she makes her call. Also tell her that you will call the agency so they will expect her call.

Let the Agency Go to Work

At this point, the role of the agent or agency is very important. This is when they do the work for which you are paying them. Let your agent step in and take control of the adoption plan, from assessing your chances for success with this particular adoption to discussing sensitive issues, such as drug and alcohol use, with the birthmother. Your agent also serves as a privacy buffer who can provide counseling services to both you and the birthparents, as well as discuss the legal aspects of your state's adoption statutes.

Your agent also needs to discuss the legal rights of the birthparents thoroughly as well as inform them about what to expect in the proceedings.

As the proceedings continue, your agent can also serve as an intermediary in ongoing communication and obtain medical records and biographical backgrounds of the birthparents, as well as oversee the in-hospital proceedings and the legal aspects of the termination of rights. He or she should also be making sure that all other state requirements are being met, such as the completion of an approved home study or filing of the application for the interim care license.

Chances are that your agent warns you on a regular basis not to set your mind on this particular match, that the birthmother can always change her mind. This is one of the great risks of parent-initiated adoption and a situation for which you can never be fully prepared.

The warning bears repeating.

Sooner or Later Your Call Will Come
Do not be surprised if a number of the phone calls you receive fall short of your expectations. For any number of reasons, the situation may not be just right for the caller to place her baby with you. The caller may not even be pregnant: she may be an interested sister, friend, or mother who is trying to convince the birthmother to make an adoption plan. If the caller is pregnant, she may decide against adoption, or she may be answering a number of adoption ads and end up choosing another prospective adopter. Sooner or later, however, a birthmother will call you and you will have an intuitive feeling that she is carrying your baby.

32

KEYS TO A SUCCESSFUL MATCH

Birthparents are as varied as the children whom they decide to place for adoption. Birthparents come from all walks of life and all social strata. There are a number of characteristics that, although not representative of all birthmothers, tend to reappear frequently enough to be considered at least somewhat common denominators among birthmothers who choose adoption.

Profile of a Birthmother Who Chooses Adoption

If she is like most women who choose to make an adoption plan, your child's birthmother is likely to be over seventeen or eighteen years old and the daughter of a working class family. She is probably unmarried and white, and she may be parenting other children. She probably has a good relationship with her father, a blue-collar worker who has had some college education. She may be in college; she at least has a vision for her own future career and education goals. At any rate, she is likely to be very mature, mature enough to know that she cannot care for a child and mature enough to consider the child's interests above her own.

Qualities Birthmothers Often Seek

In choosing adoptive parents for her child, a birthmother who is considering adoption is probably checking out a number of areas. First, she wants economic stability for her child. This is the "better life" that she knows she is unable to provide. She also wants close family ties, usually a two-parent household. She wants to feel that the parents have warmth, as well as values and interests that are similar to hers. Basically, she wants theirs to be the home that she would have provided "if things had been different."

She probably feels lucky to have the opportunity to choose the adoptive parents and hopes to have the opportunity for some degree of ongoing contact, maybe yearly photos. She may choose a particular set of parents for any number of reasons, maybe because they are an infertile couple or because they have no more than one other child in the house—maybe even because they have a shaggy dog.

Most important, she wants her child to be special in their lives.

Counseling: The Important Link

When you find an adoption situation that sounds promising, do not forget the critical importance of counseling for both you and the birthparents. Effective counseling is such an integral part of any adoption that you do not want to jeopardize your plan by omitting it.

Experts suggest that adoptive parent counseling should involve addressing your infertility issues as well as parenting skills. Birthparents need to be counseled about the losses they face through making this adoption plan. Regardless of the type of adoption you choose, adopted children need counseling as they grow to understand adoption issues themselves.

Meeting the Birthparents

If you choose an open or semiopen adoption, sometime, usually before the birth of the baby, you may have the opportunity to meet the birthmother and possibly the birthfather. Different agents have different practices for how this meeting is handled, but typically the parties meet at either the adoption agency or a neutral location, such as a restaurant, that is convenient to the birthmother. Often, the prospective adoptive couple, the professional, and the birthmother and her mother or the birthfather meet to get acquainted on an informal basis.

The situation itself is stress inducing to both prospective adopters and birthparents, all of whom who fervently want the meeting to go well. In most cases, the birthparents have already decided on adoption and have tentatively chosen the prospective adoptive parents. The meeting emparts a personal touch and a sense of kinship to the proceedings.

The agency worker probably has an agenda that includes helping the parties become acquainted, clarifying decisions about ongoing contact, reinforcing information on procedures and legalities, and making plans for in-hospital proceedings. He or she may also discuss obtaining relinquishment papers and health records from the birthfather if he chooses to be uninvolved.

It may seem to you, the prospective adoptive parent, that the birthmother is making her decision based on this meeting. This is usually not the case. By the time the actual meeting takes place, chances are good that she has already chosen you based on an intuitive feeling she had either talking to you on the telephone or reading your profile at the adoption agency. This meeting serves only to reinforce her decision. She has chosen you because she senses a commonality of beliefs or values between her family and yours. There is already a kinship of which you may not even be aware.

Tips for Increasing Your Chances for Success

Your likelihood for success in any particular adoption is influenced by any number of factors, including the following:

- The birthparents and their expectations of the adoption experience
- Your characteristics as a prospective parent
- Your expectations of the adoption experience
- The laws of your (and the birthparents') state
- Financial considerations
- Health and medical issues
- The support and approval of influential friends and family members
- Chance

If all the indicators seem to be positive, though, you can still increase your chances for a successful adoption both now, before the birth of the child, and later, when the child is a legal, active member of your family. Decisions and safeguards made now have an impact on your and your child's lifelong adoption experience.

You have probably waited a long time for the prospect of an actual adoptable child to be at hand. As compelling as it is to embrace wholeheartedly any promise of a child, though, take time to evaluate the situation and decide whether this particular situation is right for you and fits your adoption plans.

When a prospective adoption opportunity is at hand, you are at your most vulnerable. Your desire to adopt may cloud your judgment, allowing you to convince yourself of the advisability of an adoption plan that may not be suitable. As difficult as it is to let an adoption opportunity pass, other opportunities will arise. If necessary, wait and choose a situation that feels right for you.

If a particular adoption opportunity appears to be headed toward more expense than you can afford, for example, do not be afraid to let the opportunity go by while you wait for a more affordable situation.

Similarly, if the birthparents request a different degree of ongoing contact than you feel comfortable maintaining, for the sake of all the parties involved you need to wait for a situation that is more compatible with your adoption plans. A forced match may ultimately become unworkable. If you have concerns about any issues—medical, social, or legal— by all means check with your attorney or other appropriate professional and do not be afraid to pursue other options.

Part Nine

BUILDING A FAMILY THROUGH ADOPTION

Before long you will be successful in adopting a child. The uncertainty and drama of the adoption change to a vivid story, an oral history you can pass on to your child. It will become his own story of his entry into the family.

Quickly, your life will change. Like all other parents, you will wonder what life was like before your child entered your life and be thankful that you did not miss out on the opportunity to parent.

Even as a newly adoptive parent, you already know about some of the differences in adoptive families.

As a prospective adoptive parent you were in a somewhat unusual situation that only too clearly served to remind you of your infertility. Your pregnant friends had definite due dates and could count down the months in anticipation of the birth of the child. These months were spent in joyful expectation of the arrival, time that they enjoyed with baby showers, parenting classes, and decisions over birth announcements.

Your last seven or eight months, on the other hand, were probably spent quite differently. While your pregnant friends were sharing the news of their pregnancy, you were contacting adoption agents. While they were attending Lamaze classes, you were writing classified advertisements.

While they were enjoying baby showers, you were sitting at a restaurant, anxiously waiting to meet the woman you hoped to be the mother of your child.

Now that you have your child, you are probably even more aware of the differences. Your fertile friends will never have to grapple with such questions as, "What happened to my mom?" when your seven year old starts to wonder why she was adopted. They will not have to explain why another child said, "She can't be your mommy. You have slanted eyes."

Your fertile friends will never have to stumble when a new physician asks how many children they have. Their answer is the same whether the doctor is inquiring from reproductive interest or in casual conversation.

They will know the birth dates of their children. They will know where the children got their red hair and freckles or their athletic ability. They will know instinctively that the children's grandparents and relatives will give them unconditional love and acceptance. You may not know any of these things about the children who enter your family through adoption.

There will be many, many reminders of the fact that your child did not enter your family in the same manner in which most families are built.

33

FAMILY PREPARATION

Adjusting to Adoptive Parenting

Adjusting to adoptive parenting is more than getting used to instant parenting: it is accepting that your child entered your life in a way that differs from most family-building situations. It is understanding that your child comes with a heritage of his own that includes another set of parents and relatives as well as a cultural, social, and medical heritage different from your own. It is also realizing that adoption brings a whole set of issues that continue to surface as the child grows and matures in the family.

Adoptive parenting requires adjustment from other family members. Siblings must accept a newcomer who may look or act differently than they expect. Grandparents face a child who will pass on the family name without a biological connection. Even the adoptive parents themselves, after continuously reaffirming their desire to adopt, may have to overcome unrealistically high expectations for the child.

Adoptive parenting also requires sensitivity to the child's uniqueness in the family. No matter how everyone tries to make her feel the same, there are clear ways in which she differs both as an individual and as an adoptee. She may, for instance, have more contact with her birthparents than her older adopted sister has with hers. She may have physical features that set her apart from other family members. As a teen she may question her role in the family or in society based on her adopted status.

Parenting any child is a lifelong challenge. Parenting the adopted child adds a unique perspective. How many other parents, for example, struggle with telling their children that they did not enter the family in the same way most children do, or explaining why their "first" parents were not able to take care of them, or helping them grieve over their feelings of abandonment?

Many of these adoption issues come with the territory, so to speak. Others do not come to mind so readily but are nonetheless issues to which every adoptive family must learn to adjust.

For example, depending on your own adoption situation, it is a very real possibility that you have a limited medical background for your child. If you have an international child, he may have entered the United States via an international orphanage that had no access to his records. He may have arrived as a toddler without the usual round of preventive vaccines customarily given to U.S.-born infants. If your child was born in the United States, you may still be lacking a complete medical history, a tool that is especially useful in preventive health care. A person who has a predisposition to heart problems or a history of cancer, for example, is most effectively treated when his physician is aware of the genetic history and can provide early screening, diagnosis, and evaluation.

Adoption indeed entails inherent differences. As many adoptive parents teach their children, differences are neither good nor bad, but they can be an opportunity to learn and grow—with adoption in particular, a wonderful occasion that might otherwise have been missed.

Preparing Siblings and Grandparents

The degree to which you involve family members in the actual adoption process can vary. For other children already in your household, the determinants are generally the ages of the children already in the family and the situation surrounding the adoption. Young children may understand that families can be built through adoption and that a new child is coming to join the family. Older children can be more actively involved in the process.

As with the arrival of any new sibling, the children already in the household need to be aware of the changes another person will bring to the family—a baby crying at night, for example, or mom not having as much time to spend with the older children. Also, if the new child looks different from the other family members or has special needs, the other children must be aware of these differences (depending on their level of understanding) and prepared to adjust.

Older children must be aware that the newly adopted child will also have an adjustment to make. Books can be particularly beneficial in helping children learn about accepting a new brother or sister and understanding the feelings the new child will have.

Children who feel that they are an important part of the new child's welcome to the family more readily accept the new child. They can pick out new toys or help decorate the child's room, for example.

Grandparents may have a more difficult adjustment to a new adopted family member than children who are already in the household. If grandparents have not been actively involved in the adoption process, they may have difficulty understanding why you chose to adopt in the first place! Many of the same issues—genetic connectedness, for example—with which prospective adopters may grapple may be even more important to grandparents.

Grandparents may also have difficulty accepting special needs children, including children who are racially or culturally different. Their difficulties in accepting your adopted child may decrease with time and interaction with the child.

Another difficulty grandparents may have is fear that the adopted child may be reclaimed by the birthparents. Like the adoptive parents, they risk the sorrow of a birthmother's change of heart, but they also fear the heartbreak their own child would have to endure.

You can help prepare your parents for adoptive grandparenting by sharing information and discussing adoption issues with them. Some adoptive parents have found a gift subscription to an adoptive parent newsletter to be helpful for newly adoptive grandparents.

34

EASING THE CHILD'S TRANSITION

As difficult as the transition of an adopted child into the household is for adoptive parents and siblings, the transition is more difficult for the adopted child. Even an infant experiences the stress of a disruption of routine and the presence of unfamiliar sights, sounds, and smells in the new home.

International children or children who are older, who have experienced multiple foster (and adoptive) placements, or who have been abused are particularly vulnerable to the stresses of a new adoptive home. These children must adjust to new routines and new relationships, and, for international children, new language, foods, and customs.

Adoption is a major change in a child's life. The child who is entering your family through adoption is most likely breaking old attachments with people who have been important in her life, and she is being expected to build new attachments. It is important that you help your child with her transition to her new adoptive home.

There are a number of ways that you can help your child adjust to his or her new home and family:

- Schedule individual and family counseling. Counseling is imperative if you are adopting a child who has suffered from one or more broken attachments or who has experienced abuse. Your child will have separation and bereavement issues to deal with whether she is being separated from her biological family, an interim care home, or an orphanage. An abused or neglected child may have difficulty forming attachments or may exhibit acting out behaviors for any number of reasons.

- Make a life book with your child. By helping your child put together a memory book about his life both before and after adoptive placement, you help him express and accept his feelings about the different segments of his life. Pictures and drawings that he chooses to include will help him bridge the gap from his early experiences to his new life. He can include drawings and stories of birthparents, foster parents, siblings, adoptive parents, and any other significant individuals in his life. In addition to recording memories, a life book helps to show that life after adoption is a continuation of all the child's lifetime experiences, not a replacement for them.
- Provide opportunities for your child to learn about and experience her birth culture. Adoption advocates stress the importance of helping adopted children maintain a cultural connectedness to their heritage, particularly if this heritage is vastly different from that of their adopted family or their peers. You can help your child by valuing her cultural background—serving native dishes, for example—and by introducing her to children who have the same physical features and background as she does. Many adoptive families find a cultural connectedness for their children through adoptive family support groups or culture camps in which children with like heritages can meet and form friendships.
- Intervene on his behalf. As an adoptive parent, there will be times when it is necessary for you to advocate for your child. For example, if your ten-year-old child who was

adopted internationally is not capable of fifth grade work in a U.S. school, you need to access community resources to help him adjust. Do not place him in the second grade, as some well-intentioned school officials may suggest, and hope for the best.
- Provide suitable books on adoption and adoptive families. A number of good, sensitive books are available for children. The books present a wide variety of adoption issues, from acceptance of differences to adjusting to a new family. Written for a wide range of ages, these books deal with many types of families built through adoption.
- Have realistic expectations. Your child's adjustment will not be without difficulty. If you are knowledgeable about the experiences your child has encountered in the past, understand the issues related to her transition, and prepared to help her weather the difficulties, you will greatly increase your chances for success.

35

INSURANCE, BENEFITS, AND SUBSIDIES

For many years, adoptive families have been at a disadvantage in obtaining medical coverage and other company benefits for their adopted children. Until recently, employers frequently did not offer the same benefits to their employees who adopted children as they provided to their employees who gave birth.

Major changes have taken place and continue to take place, however. An important breakthrough occurred when the U.S. Congress passed the Omnibus Budget Reconciliation Act of 1993. This law mandates that, with some qualification, all employer group health plans that provide coverage for dependent children of participants must cover adopted children from the time of placement for adoption. The law also prohibits restriction of coverage because of a preexisting condition the child may have and supercedes state laws that may allow lesser coverage for adopted children.

Before this legislation, unless otherwise mandated by state laws, insurance companies were free to limit coverage on adopted children. Adoptive parents were forced to purchase expensive coverage elsewhere, if it was available at all. Ultimately some adoptions, especially for children with special needs, were not completed at all because of the inaccessibility of health insurance.

Other adoption benefits have been developed or expanded in recent years. A growing number of companies offer an adoption benefits plan to their employees. Such a plan commonly offers financial assistance or reimbursement to assist employees in adoption-related expenses and provides adoptive parent leave (frequently a combination of paid and unpaid leave similar to maternity and paternity leave) for adoptive parent employees. A company's financial assistance plan may provide reimbursement for specific adoption expenses or for a set monetary limit. Covered expenses typically include agency fees, legal fees, medical expenses, and pregnancy expenses for the birthmother.

In addition, a growing number of companies are helping their employees access information about adoption. The companies contract with a human resources firm that helps the employee obtain information about adoption issues, such as the process of adoption, types of adoption, agents and agencies, and international adoption.

Beyond company-sponsored adoption benefits plans, other adoption benefits programs are also available. These include (1) state reimbursement for adoption expenses and subsidies for special needs adoptions, and (2) military reimbursements for adoption expenses for military families.

State reimbursements are generally provided for one-time adoption expenses for waiting children. State laws vary with regard to the amount of financial assistance and regulation for reimbursement. In some adoption cases, financial assistance is also available to help offset ongoing expenses in caring for special needs children. If you are considering adopting a waiting child who may be eligible for assistance, it is imperative that you ask about such subsidies before adoptive placement, though, since application for these monies is commonly not accepted after placement.

Military families are also eligible for reimbursement for certain adoption-related expenses. The Defense Authorization Bill of 1991 provides reimbursement for up to $2,000 to help cover the costs of an infant, international, or waiting child adoption by a military family.

Part Ten

BEYOND THE PROCESS OF ADOPTION

If you adopt an infant, his or her discharge from the hospital—the first breaking of ties with the birthmother—is one milestone, but this event takes only a matter of days. The wait for the next milestone, termination of rights, is much longer. In both situations, your powerlessness is painfully apparent.

Infant or older child adoption, the uncertainty of waiting for the final steps may be stressful for the adoptive parents. As threatening as the time may seem to the adoptive parents, however, this period is an important, exciting time in your child's life—a time that you will want to remember and share over and over in the retelling of your child's personal history.

As the legal process of adoption unfolds you will undoubtedly experience a growing sense of entitlement to your child. Feelings of insecurity about parenting are replaced by confidence. Feelings of gratitude for having this child in your life are replaced by a conviction that no other child could replace your child and, most important, that this is indeed your child.

Eventually, the legal milestones are replaced by emotional milestones that serve to remind you of the child's entry into your life—his birthday, anniversaries of his arrival date, Mother's Day, and Father's Day.

If you adopted an older child, the milestones that touch your heart will come from the child herself. The legal milestones are still valid and important, but your child's acceptance of you as a genuine parent will be the most important measure.

Later, your child's achievements will serve as milestones—completion of the first set of swimming lessons, Sunday school graduation, first day of kindergarten, and many, many others to follow.

36

BONDING AND ENTITLEMENT

Two important concerns in adoptive family building are bonding and entitlement. *Bonding* is the development of a close parent-child relationship. *Entitlement* extends beyond a parent assuming legal responsibility for the welfare of a child: it includes a feeling that the parent has a spiritual right to love, nurture, and protect the welfare of the child.

In the past, many people felt that true bonding with a child must begin at birth (or, preferably, prenatally) and occurs only between parents and their biologically conceived children. This belief gave rise to, among other trends, the current emphasis on a father's active participation in the birthing experience. Until recently, little credence was given to the bonding ability of individuals who are not related by blood or to those blood relatives who did not experience early bonding. Both experience and common sense have disproved this theory for biologically built families as well as adoptive families; however, the myth remains strong among some people that adoptive families lack the benefit of a bonding experience. It is true that parent-child closeness does not always develop instantaneously between a parent and the adopted child, but neither does this closeness miraculously develop between a biologically conceived child and parent. Bonding is a gradual feeling of love and caring rather than an emotion-packed moment of discovery.

Adoptive parents also often struggle with feelings of entitlement for their child, especially when the adoptive parents have developed a close relationship with the birthparent(s). It is not uncommon for newly adoptive parents to feel more like caretakers than actual parents to their child. Like bonding, entitlement frequently tends to be gradual.

A number of issues related to adoptive parenting may delay or interfere with your development of a sense of bonding with or, later, entitlement to your newly adopted child. These include the following:

- The stresses of infertility
- The rigors of finding an adoption agency
- The drama of finding an adoptable child
- The indecision of waiting
- The life changes that accompany the presence of a new person in your life
- Difficult behaviors the child may exhibit in reaction to the new environment
- The differences and sense of mystery your child brings to the extended family
- Your feelings about your child's history and birthparents
- The normal stresses of parenting
- The initial lack of permanency in the parent-child relationship

Your child's entry into your life, although it may or may not have followed the pattern of a typical adoption, is different from the arrival of a biologically conceived child whose anticipated entry in the family is heralded by traditional welcoming events: announcement of pregnancy, baby showers, doctor appointments, labor, and childbirth.

The biologically conceived baby is accepted without hesitation as a child, grandchild, and niece or nephew. No one wonders about his past or his role in the family. No one questions what negative traits she may have inherited from her "other" parents or if those "other" parents will ever lay claim to her.

As an adoptive parent you are denied the rituals associated with pregnancy and childbirth. Instead, you are forced to shield your child from the negative perceptions of society about adoption and adopted children. Also, you are likely to experience a wide range of emotions about your child's birthparents and history. In an infant adoption, for example, these feelings may include gratitude to the birthparents for making an adoption plan for the child (and quite possibly choosing you to parent the child) and sympathy for the birthparents who leave the hospital childless. In a special needs adoption, your emotions may include resentment of the birthparents for somehow preventing the child from enjoying a carefree childhood.

Grappling with these myriad issues may delay your feeling a complete bonding with or entitlement to your child, as, for example, initially feeling that you are playing the role of caretaker rather than parent to your child. The feelings may surface as questioning the decision to adopt or your ability to love a child who is not your flesh and blood.

As stressful as these uncertainties are, they are not uncommon. New parents, whether adoptive or biological, often question their decision and ability to parent. With time and counseling, if appropriate, most parents feel a closeness to their children and a parent-child bond develops that makes them wonder why they ever doubted their capacity to love and their ability to nurture. With time, feelings of entitlement evolve.

Some adoptive parents truly believe in the religious influence of adoption, that a higher power brought their child to them. Others believe in a more earthly approach, that they had the innate ability to parent no matter how the child came to them. No matter what your beliefs about why your child entered your life, if you are like most adoptive parents, you feel the sense of kinship with and entitlement to your child.

37

COPING WITH DISAPPOINTMENT

Birthmother Decides to Parent

Undoubtedly one of the most devastating aspects of infant adoption is the possibility that at any point before the termination of parental rights, the birthmother may change her mind and decide to parent the child.

Through an unfortunate chain of events, one Midwest couple experienced two such changes of heart in one weekend. Working through a well-known adoption attorney, the couple had provided financial support to a pregnant woman during the last few months of her pregnancy. Although the adoption was confidential and their attorney had warned of the birthmother's right to reconsider, the couple was naturally enthused about the sincerity of the birthmother to place the child and the impending birth.

"We hadn't met the birthmother, but she chose us from profiles our attorney provided. We felt very comfortable with this situation, so we were terribly disappointed to learn that she had decided to take the baby home with her from the hospital," the prospective adoptive mother explained.

Less than two days later, a baby was born to another birthmother who had been working through the same adoption attorney. Like the previous birthmother, the second birthmother had selected an adoptive couple from the attorney's files. After the birth of the child, though, the couple the second birthmother had chosen unexplainedly backed out of the arrangement.

"We don't know what happened to make the other couple change their minds, but our attorney showed our profile to the second birthmother. She seemed to like us, but I guess it was hard for her to get over the disappointment of the first couple. She decided to parent the baby," the disappointed prospective adoptive mother said.

Four months later, the couple adopted another birthmother's baby girl.

Estimates vary about the number of birthmothers who, despite nondirective counseling and seemingly sincere intentions, change their minds and decide to parent their children. A visit to any adoptive parent support group or adoption professional is sure to reconfirm the real potentiality that changes of heart may and do occur regularly in adoption planning.

No one can tell you how to react if such a situation occurs in your adoption plan. For couples who have struggled with infertility issues, who have spent years on adoption agency rosters, and who question the eventual placement of any child in their lives, a birthmother's change of heart can be devastating.

If this eventuality happens in your adoption plan, it is certainly not uncommon for you to experience the various stages of grieving—denial, anger, bargaining, depression, and acceptance—that others feel after a significant loss. Even though your loss seems to be less concrete than a physical loss through death, for instance, you are nonetheless sensing the loss of your dreams and hopes for family and completeness.

Your adoption professional, grief counselor, or adoptive parent support group may be able to assist you. You may also be able to take comfort knowing that many other parents have successfully adopted despite similar disappointments.

Disruption and Dissolution

Despite your best intentions and preparations to parent an adopted child, terminations do occur and the child is returned to the adoption agency. These include *disruptions* (the adoption is terminated before finalization) and *dissolutions* (the adoption is terminated after finalization). Estimates vary about their frequency, but terminations tend to be more frequent among older adopted children, particularly those who have had multiple placements, and relatively uncommon in infant adoption.

When adoptions reach the stage of termination, it is often caused by a disparity in expectations: the parent expects something the child cannot give or the child gives something the parent did not expect. The cause is generally attributed to three factors that may or may not be present in individual cases: (1) incomplete or incorrect information is provided to adopters, often by adoption workers eager to make an adoptive placement, (2) the stresses of adoption, and (3) the adoptee's traumatic history of abuse and broken attachments.

Despite access to accurate background information and the availability of counseling services and agency support systems, however, some adoptive situations continue to be desperate and lead to terminations. The unfortunate victims are both the adoptive parents and the child.

Birth Defects

Many adoptive parents believe that, after the birth of the child and the birthmother's action to place the child for adoption, the child is theirs legally, emotionally, and spiritually. No physical complications, such as disease or birth defects, will keep them from accepting the child and parenting her as their own.

Other prospective parents feel that, for any number of reasons—emotional and physical stress, limited financial resources, or preconceived expectations—they are only capable of dealing with certain birth complications.

Regardless of how you feel about the acceptability of birth defects, it is important for you to come to terms with your feelings and discuss them in advance with your adoption agent. Since the primary concern of adoption professionals is the welfare of the child, no one will force you to accept a child for whom you do not feel capable of caring.

38

SPEAKING POSITIVELY ABOUT ADOPTION

Historically, the words and phrases used to describe adoption and the individuals involved resounded with negative undertones. For example, birthparents were thought to be irresponsible and uncaring, their choice about adoption was between "giving up" the children or "keeping" them, and regardless of the choice, the children were labeled illegitimate.

Consider the consequences of this negatively charged language. How do children feel when the circumstances of their early lives are spoken of in such uncaring terms? What does it say about the children's birthparents, who are trying to make one of the hardest, most responsible decisions in their lives?

When the same situation is described in different words—birthparents deciding between making an adoption plan or choosing to parent—a different feeling about the process is conveyed. Merely by changing terminology, language conveys respect for the birthparents, empathy for the difficulty of their choice, and admiration for their concern about their children, whether or not they ultimately choose adoption.

Notice, too, how frequently the fact of a person's adopted status becomes significant in conversation: "They've had trouble with that young man ever since he was young. They adopted him as an infant. They never knew what they were getting into." Such language places the entire blame for the young man's troubles on his adoptive status, overlooking the fact that hundreds of thousands of parents have difficulty with their biological children.

In the past, when adoption was veiled in secrecy and birthmothers were considered unfit and uncaring, the language of adoption reflected these attitudes. Today, a new understanding of adoption has focused attention on a more humane approach to adoption issues.

The use of new, positive language about adoption is very important. Words carry tremendous impact. It is important to have this force positively influence the lives of adopted children. Adoptive parents and adoption advocates must work together to continue to increase public awareness about adoption issues.

Fortunately, a new language has been developed that reflects this sensitivity to adoption. This new language, known as positive adoption language (PAL), is nonjudgmental, emphasizes the positive aspects of adoption as a method of family building, and stresses the importance of choice, sensitivity, and understanding.

The following is a list of some of the antiquated, judgmental terms used to describe adoption matched with the preferred PAL terms:

KEYS TO ADOPTING A CHILD

Antiquated, Judgmental Terms	*Positive Adoption Language*
Real, natural parents	Birthparents
Surrender, relinquish, give up for adoption	Make an adoption plan
Keep the child	Choose to parent
Hard to place children	Waiting (or special needs) children
Handicapped children	Children with disabilities
Available children	Adoptable children
"The child is adopted"	"The child was adopted"
Foreign adoption	International adoption
Reunion (with real parents)	Meeting with birthparents
Home study	Parent preparation

39

A TRUE STORY FOR NONTRADITIONAL ADOPTERS

My husband and I decided to adopt later in life. We were both in our early forties, well into a second marriage and with twenty-year-old twins in college. A hysterectomy in my twenties had prevented me from bearing children but not from enjoying these two stepchildren since they were eleven. It was not until years later, though, after Tony had finished five years of evening law school, that we discussed adoption with any degree of seriousness.

With twenty years of child-raising experience under his belt, Tony was strongly in favor of adopting an infant rather than an older child. Although I was afraid of the demands of such a young child, he wanted me to experience the joys of a newborn child. With his preferences in mind, I started my search. I contacted every adoption agency I heard about, only to get the same response: too many couples, not enough babies.

Yet my intuition told me that there was more to adoption than what was widely known. The media reported on adoption often enough, usually either accounts of black market babies or "human interest" stories of demoralized couples who had been unsuccessful in obtaining a baby. I was sure that there was an untold story, though, one that had a happy ending.

Basically we faced two constraints: time and money. Since at that time we lived in one of the few states that prohibited independent adoption, most adopters waited out lengthy stints on agency lists. We did not feel we could afford the six or seven year wait that was typical of an infant adoption. We investigated international adoption only to find that we were beyond the age limit many countries would allow for an infant adoption. We did not have the personal finances that would allow us to contact an independent adoption lawyer in another state, or did we feel we had the patience to tackle the challenges of a waiting child.

As a result, I had to do my homework to find some alternatives. One of these alternatives involved locating a birthmother on our own. When I first mentioned the idea to Tony, he felt uncomfortable with the suggestion. "I don't think it's a good idea for a birthmother to know much about us," he explained. As I learned more, I found that some parent-initiated adoptions do not include complete disclosure, that, in fact, many are completed without the birthparents having any identifying information about the prospective adoptive parents.

When Tony tentatively agreed to pursue this idea as one alternative, I found an in-state agency that was innovative in finding birthmothers who wanted to make an adoption plan and willing to work with couples who were agreeable to trying alternatives, such as locating birthmothers on their own. They agreed to work with us as we independently advertised for a birthmother.

Meanwhile, I started thinking about the benefits of having an opportunity for ongoing accessibility to the

A TRUE STORY FOR NONTRADITIONAL ADOPTERS

birthmother, especially the benefits to the adopted child. I had been concerned about the natural curiosity of an adopted child, how he would have questions about his heritage and his birthparents. I thought that if we, his parents, knew about his birthparents and were comfortable with discussing these issues, our child would be spared anxiety and guilt feelings about wanting to learn more about himself.

We started our advertising plan with a classified ad in a number of small weekly papers, an ad typical of many that we had noticed in large daily newspapers: "Loving couple seeks to adopt healthy infant." We ran the advertisement for four weeks, inviting interested birthmothers to call us collect. The phone number on the ad was for a second line that we had installed and kept unlisted. (Although we were aware that we might receive prank or moralistic phone calls, we never did.)

Each weekly ad did draw interest although sometimes it was merely from other would-be adoptive couples wanting to find out about the success of our ads. Other responses came from either pregnant women who were considering adoption and examining their alternatives or their concerned relatives who advocated adoption.

One birthmother seemed very interested; in fact, she told me that we were the answer to her prayers. After a very pleasant chat on the phone, I explained that the next step was for her to contact our agency to set up a time for us to meet. She gave me her phone number and promised to call the agency in the morning. She called the agency as promised and planned to call the social worker back with a date when we could meet. She never made the next phone call. Our attempts to reach her proved unsuccessful. Both the number she had given us and a different phone number and address she had given to the agency social worker were fictitious.

After trying to analyze the results we were receiving from the ads, I decided to try a different, more personal approach. The new ad read as follows:

ADOPTION

> Would you like your child to grow up with ponies, storybooks, and close family ties? We would like to adopt a baby. We are working with a licensed state agency that offers openness in adoption and counseling services. If you'd like more information, please call collect, XXX-XXXX.

Once again, we received only a smattering of calls, dead-end responses that discouraged us to the point of silent despair. I remember telling Tony that I would never recommend advertising for birthparents to any but the most strongly resolved. This course of raised and dashed hopes was taking its toll on us.

Our one salvation against hopelessness was the knowledge that we had other options. Our agency was still advertising for birthmothers, and we were still, albeit slowly, working our way up their list. We also decided that if we did not find a baby by the end of the summer, we would pursue a legal risk adoption, with the plan of providing interim care for a preselected baby, one who would be likely to have adoption as a part of her permanent placement plan.

Our agency was, in fact, finding birthmothers. Along with the other couples who completed the screening process, we compiled a profile booklet about ourselves. These booklets were made available to birthmothers who had the option of choosing a family for their child. The usual procedure was that a birthmother was offered the profiles of the couples who had worked their way into the top ten places on the list. Since our number was forty-four when we

A TRUE STORY FOR NONTRADITIONAL ADOPTERS

completed the requirements, we knew that a certain number of months would elapse before our profile was even shown to a birthmother.

Slowly we crept up the list.

Then, on the day we returned from a midwinter vacation to Key West, we found a message on the tape machine connected to the baby phone. With my by then conditioned apprehension, I reached for the phone.

Anne was a woman in her late thirties who told me that her daughter, who was due the following month, was considering adoption. My heart pounded as I waved Tony toward the phone. "It's real," I whispered to him.

I told Anne about us, about the services the agency provided, and a little of what I knew about openness options in adoption. She replied that such an adoption plan seemed to be what her daughter was hoping for.

Soon I was talking to Darcy herself on the phone. My heart raced.

Darcy was twenty. She had moved into an apartment with a friend shortly after graduating from high school. She met a young man and they started dating. Not long after, they went to Darcy's parents to tell them that she was pregnant.

Darcy dreamed of parenting the baby and eventually marrying Bill. Even when he told her that he wanted to date other girls, she continued to wait, expecting him to change his mind and renew his commitment to her and the child. Months later, Darcy finally accepted that Bill was not going to change his mind—not ready to parent, not ready to make a commitment. As a minimum wage worker, Darcy foresaw the difficulties of raising a child as a single parent. She began to think about adoption.

Darcy wanted her child to have the best that life had to offer, and to her this meant that her child would have a mother and a father. She approached her mother about the idea of making an adoption plan.

As Darcy talked, Anne agreed that adoption seemed to be the best alternative. She showed Darcy our ad, which she had saved, tucked away in a dresser drawer.

Darcy asked her mother to call us.

Even on the phone Darcy was upbeat and positive. She was as determined a twenty year old as they come. In the few minutes that we talked on the phone, she decided that we were the couple whom she wanted to parent her unborn child. Both Darcy and her mom had been attracted to the ad, she told me, because "it seemed as though it talked about the things that our family likes to do."

I couldn't help but like her. She was so fresh and honest. I could tell that she cared enough about that unborn baby to be able to field the blows of derision she might encounter when telling her friends and relatives that she had decided to make an adoption plan.

We ended the call with Darcy agreeing to call our agency the next day to set up an appointment to meet us.

The next day Tony called the agency to inform them that Darcy would be calling.

Darcy did not call. She did not call the following day. On the third day, Tony called Mrs. Parker, our social worker and head of the agency, to ask her to call Darcy. We were relieved to hear that Mrs. Parker had reached Anne at home earlier that day and, yes, Darcy still wanted to make an adoption plan and she still wanted us to parent her child.

A TRUE STORY FOR NONTRADITIONAL ADOPTERS

Mrs. Parker told Anne a little about the agency and its procedures and agreed to send Darcy some information about adoption and our agency's services. She also promised to include papers for the baby's birthfather to complete regarding his medical history and his agreement to termination of his parental rights to the baby. The next step, Mrs. Parker told Anne, was for Anne and Darcy to set up a time when they would like to meet with us.

A week passed but no call from Darcy.

Then, late on a Tuesday afternoon, Mrs. Parker called to ask if we could get together that Friday to meet Darcy and her mother. Darcy had called the agency earlier in the day. Her doctor had advised her that the baby had dropped and added that she should not be traveling more than an hour's distance away from home.

This restriction necessitated that both Mrs. Parker and we drive to Darcy's hometown to meet with her rather than at the agency, where most of their adoption meetings take place.

Our sense of trepidation intensified over the course of the week, so that by Friday we had exhausted ourselves over decisions on what to wear, what to say, and how to act. We knew that Darcy liked us and that we had gotten along exceptionally well with both her and Anne, but the nagging insecurities ravaged us: Would we pass the ultimate human test of being chosen to raise another woman's child?

We arrived in town in plenty of time to locate the restaurant where we would meet and the hospital where Darcy would be delivering. We also had time to check out available lodging for our stay when Darcy and the baby were in the hospital. All that, and we still had an hour and a half to kill.

The time finally came for us to go into the restaurant. Once inside, we took turns using the restroom, continuously reminding ourselves of everyone's names. We drank coffee and tried to converse.

Right on schedule, Darcy, Anne, and Mrs. Parker, who had met each other in the parking lot, entered the restaurant. Their parking lot meeting had broken the ice so that our introductions seemed relaxed and friendly from the start.

Despite her youth, Darcy made everyone feel as though we were there for one purpose: to set the course for the best possible future for an unborn child. Darcy had already made her choice. We were the parents whom she wanted to raise her child.

Darcy showed us pictures of herself and her family and told us more about her plans for the future. She had already told her family, friends, and coworkers about her decision to make an adoption plan for the baby. When they questioned her, she told us, she explained that the baby needed a mother and a father. At her young age and lacking training for a well-paying job, she knew that she could not give a baby the care and attention he needed. The baby's father, she added, had agreed to provide medical information and to sign the papers necessary for termination of rights.

I asked Darcy if there was a little gift or memento that she would like to give the baby for us to keep until he was older. Yes, there were some pictures she would like him to have, and maybe her mother could knit a baby blanket for him for the trip home from the hospital.

"I can't think of anything nicer," I replied. "This is so wonderful—just the thought of being able to tell the baby what a kind, happy family he came from."

Only the technicalities remained. Mrs. Parker gave Darcy our profile to look through at her leisure and then talked with her about her legal rights and what to expect. When Darcy and the baby were to be discharged from the hospital, Mrs. Parker explained, the baby would be released to the agency for interim care. He would then be transferred to us as interim care providers. The next day, she would petition the court in Darcy's county for a date for termination of rights. At that hearing, Darcy would go before the judge and state that the release of her child was her true intent. After that, Darcy would have 21 days to appeal the court ruling. Then the child would be legally in our care for the purposes of adoption, a process that would take the following year to complete.

The baby was due a week after our meeting. Without hesitation, Darcy invited us to visit both her and the baby in the hospital. Anne assured us that she would call us when Darcy was headed for the hospital.

The details of that meeting will be forever etched in my mind. When we left the restaurant an hour and a half later, I could remember no experience that had been as comfortable and comforting.

All that remained was the phone call from Anne. The week passed slowly. And the following week.

Tony called Mrs. Parker, asking how she deals with anxious fathers. "Babies take their time," she replied good-naturedly.

Three days later he called Darcy.

"I feel like a blimp," she joked, "and the doctor's not much help. All he says is 'It's still in there.'"

"We just wanted to call and find out how you were feeling," he said. "I'll bet you'll be glad to be on your way to the hospital."

"I sure will. Mom will call you when we leave. I hope it's soon!"

I could feel Tony's relief as he ended the call. Yes, everything was still fine. Darcy was still pregnant. She still planned to follow through on her adoption plan. We were still her choice.

Four nights later we got Anne's call. Darcy was going to the hospital.

Already half-packed, we needed only half an hour before we were on the road. When we arrived in Havertown three hours later, we called the hospital. Darcy had delivered a baby boy an hour earlier.

We tried to wait patiently the one hour until visiting hours began. Tentatively we climbed the stairs to the maternity ward.

"Can I help you?" a pleasant gray-haired nurse asked.

"Uh, we're adopting the Nelson baby," we stammered.

"He's down in the room with Darcy. I'll take you there."

A look of apprehension passed between us, but our anxiety quickly dissipated when we saw Darcy.

"Come on in," she smiled. "Look at him."

Then softly to her little son, "Meet your new mom and dad."

For the next two days, we visited both the baby and Darcy in her hospital room. We knew Darcy needed time to sort through her feelings about the baby, about herself, and about her choice.

"I'm not going to tell the baby's father about his birth until after both of us are discharged. I want you well on your way with the baby. He signed the papers already and said that he didn't want to come to the hospital, so I'll just tell him later."

On the day we were to take the baby home, Mrs. Parker met us at the hospital.

"I'm going to go in and talk to Darcy and Anne, and then I'll come back and get you," she explained. "There's some paperwork she'll have to sign releasing the baby to interim care."

We sat silently in the nurses' lounge, both wondering if we had come that far to be successful in our hopes of adopting a baby. Although we had seemed to overcome hurdle after hurdle, we could not help but wonder what would happen next.

When Mrs. Parker came back to get us, she walked with us down to Darcy's room. All packed and ready to go home, Darcy held the baby in her arms as we entered. The little gifts her friends and relatives had brought the baby were piled neatly beside the bed. The child was wrapped in the blanket Anne had made for him.

Almost ceremoniously, Darcy handed the baby to Tony.

I hugged Anne and whispered, "Thank you," knowing that without Anne's support, Darcy might not have had the emotional courage to pursue her best instincts for that little baby.

When I hugged Darcy I thanked her for having chosen us, "I hope we can live up to the trust that you've placed in us."

On the day we brought our little son home from the hospital, we could barely believe that he was, in fact, soon to be ours. We had forgotten the anxieties of raised hopes and dashed dreams. Our nine month wait for a child seemed pitifully short.

Darcy went to court two weeks after the baby's discharge from the hospital. Dannie was legally placed in our home for the purpose of adoption twenty-one days later.

Although Darcy had asked only for yearly photos and an opportunity to meet Dannie when he is an adult, if he desires, we continue to exchange photos and notes every few months. At first I was unsure whether the additional contact would be a gift or an added burden to her. When I asked, she responded in her usual upbeat manner, "I love seeing the pictures and hearing how he's doing. It makes me sure that I made the right decision."

QUESTIONS AND ANSWERS

Why is the adoption process so expensive and lengthy?

Customarily, prospective adoptive parents pay all legal adoption-related expenses. These expenses are paid either directly to birthparents through reimbursements through an adoption intermediary or indirectly through agency fees. (Costs may be partially offset by the birthparents' access to medical coverage, donations to adoption agencies, such as United Way contributions, or state subsidies.) Legally reimbursable expenses vary from state to state; they may or may not include medical expenses, prescriptions, hospital charges, counseling fees, rent, and clothing allotments for the birthmother. Additional costs that adopters may incur include fees for such services as legal representation and counseling, as well as travel and advertising expenses.

Adoptions vary considerably in the length of time between application and placement. The main factor that influences the waiting time for an adoption is demand for a particular type of adoptable child; there is generally a longer wait for a white newborn, for example, than for a special needs child. Sometimes the adoptions of waiting children are lengthy because of agency understaffing. Screening procedures and parent preparation classes for adoptive parents add to the length of time necessary to complete an adoption.

How realistic is adoption as a way of family building for nontraditional adopters?

If you are creative, willing to educate yourself on the adoption process, and open to new approaches to adoption, your chances are good. Start by joining an adoptive parents support group, particularly one that includes nontraditional adopters who have been successful at adoption. They can give you ideas on how to proceed. You may have to investigate the availability of adoptable children in developing nations, for example, or try novel approaches to classified advertising for birthparents. Your chances of successfully adopting are very good. The vast majority of prospective adopters who are persistent do adopt.

Does the value of permanence in a child's life outweigh the anguish of prejudice for a child adopted transracially?

The National Association of Black Social Workers strongly supports the importance of black children being raised by black families. They argue against transracial adoption. Others disagree. This must be an individual decision based on the environment in which your child will be raised and the support and guidance in dealing with prejudice that you can offer your child.

What safeguards does an adopter have against a birthparent's change of heart and reclaiming the child?

A birthparent has the right to decide to parent the child (for any reason) until the court has terminated parental rights. After that time, the birthparent must show that her rights were violated in some manner for her to reclaim the child. Your best safeguard is to work with a reputable, experienced agent (who will advise you that there are no guarantees), to know and abide by the laws of the state(s) that have jurisdiction, and to insist that counseling services be available for the birthparents. Your only real protection is not to take custody of a child until she is legally free for adoption, a process that may take many months.

Am I selfish to want to adopt a healthy, same-race infant?

Many adopters feel pressured to adopt a waiting child. Perhaps the pressure comes from adoption advocates who value permanent placement for waiting children or from social workers who are pressured to find homes for waiting children. You are not selfish in wanting to adopt a healthy same-race infant. What is important is your ability to love and nurture the child.

Can a child be adopted out of state to avoid the strict regulations of an adopter's home state?

No. This is a foolhardy approach that, although tempting, jeopardizes your adoption. Out-of-state adoptions must be approved by adoption officials in both states.

GLOSSARY

Adoptable children children who are legally free for adoption
Adoption agency an agency authorized by a state licensing board to complete adoptions in that state
Adoption agent see *Adoption professional*
Adoption circle key members of an adoption unit: birthparents, adoptive parents, and adoptee
Adoption professional an adoption worker (generally an attorney or social worker) who is authorized by a state licensing board to complete adoptions in that state
Adoptive parent leave a leave of absence from a place of employment for the purposes of adopting a child
Assisted reproduction the use of donated eggs or sperm to conceive a child or carry a child
Attention deficit disorder a physical condition characterized by the patient's inability to concentrate on a specific task for long periods of time
Best interest of the child a legal principle that dictates that the child's welfare be a determinant in decisions concerning adoption
Biologically built family a family in which the child(ren) has been biologically conceived by both parents
Birthparents the set of parents who conceived a child
Black any child of mainly African descent
Bonding the development of a close parent-child relationship
Child-free life-style a life in which the participant(s) do not parent either biological or adopted children

GLOSSARY

Children of color any child of African, Hispanic, Native American, East Indian, and/or Asian descent

Confidential adoption an adoption of a child between anonymous birthparents and adopters, which may involve the exchange of nonidentifying information, such as medical and social histories about the child

Contingency plan a secondary, or backup plan in the event that the primary adoption plan does not prove to be workable

Cultural heritage the set of customs, traditions, language, and, frequently, religion shared by a group of people

Defense Authorization Bill of 1991 a plan that provides reimbursement for eligible military personnel to help defray the costs of an adoption

Disruption an interruption to the adoption process in which the adoption is terminated before finalization

Dissolution an interruption to the adoption process in which the adoption is terminated after finalization

Domestic adoption an adoption of a child who is a citizen of the United States

Donor insemination an infertility procedure in which a male provides fertile semen to be used in an attempt to conceive a child

Egg donation an infertility procedure in which a female provides a fertile egg to be used in an attempt to conceive a child

Entitlement a parent's feeling to be a rightful provider of love, guidance, and care to a child

Fost/adopt see *Legal risk adoption*

Genetic connection a biological relationship to a child

Home study see *Parent preparation*

Identified adoption a self-directed adoption plan in which birth and adoptive parents make use of an adoption agency to complete an adoption plan

Independent (private) adoption an adoption assisted by an adoption agent as opposed to an agency adoption
Indian Child Welfare Act of 1978 a federal law governing the placement of children of Native American descent
Infertile the inability to conceive a child
Infertility treatment medical treatments aimed at enabling a participant to conceive a child
Interim care temporary residential custodial care of a child in a nonrelated family setting
International adoption the legal adoption of children who are not U.S. citizens
International children children who are not citizens of the United States
Interstate adoption the legal adoption of children who are not residents of the same state as the adopter
Interstate Compact on the Placement of Children a legal agreement that governs all interstate adoptions
Joint creation the conception of a child that results from the joining of sperm and egg of two parenting partners
Jurisdiction the authority or territory empowered to interpret and apply the law
Legal Risk Adoption (fost/adopt) the situation in which a child is placed in the temporary custody of a prospective adoptive couple before the child is legally free for adoption
Life book a collection of photographs, drawings, and keepsakes that helps an adopted child link his or her life before and after adoption
Networking an informal, usually verbal, procedure of notifying friends and acquaintances of your desire to adopt
Nonidentifying contact interaction between birth and prospective adoptive parents in which identifying information is not shared
Nontraditional adopter any prospective adoptive parent who does not fit the traditional adopter's profile

Omnibus Budget Reconciliation Act of 1993 a federal law that mandates that, with some qualification, all employer group health plans must provide coverage for dependent adopted children of participants from the time of placement for adoption

Open adoption a style of adoption characterized by full disclosure of identifying information and an agreement to maintain ongoing contact between birth and adoptive parents

Orphanage a group home intended to house homeless or abandoned children

Parent-initiated (self-directed) adoption an adoption plan in which birthparents or prospective adoptive parents take an active role in locating parties interested in completing an adoption plan; frequently the parties meet and formulate plans for the adoption before enlisting the help of an adoption professional

Parent preparation an instructional program designed to teach parenting skills to adoptive parents

Peer group people of similar age and common interests

Permanency an opportunity for a child to establish a long-lasting relationship as part of a family unit

Photolisting book a booklet of photographs and short narratives that identifies waiting children who are legally free for adoption

Positive adoption language (PAL) nonjudgmental terminology that emphasizes the positive aspects of adoption as a method of family building

Profile of prospective adopter a written description of a prospective adoptive parent, usually prepared by the prospective adopter and offered to birthparents by adoption agents as a tool to assist birthparents in selecting an adoptive parent for their child

Profile of waiting children a written description of the physical characteristics, behaviors, and history of an adoptable child

Prospective adoptive parents singles, married couples, or parenting couples seeking to adopt a child

Screening (birth or prospective adoptive parents) an evaluative measure used to determine the suitability of an individual as a prospective member of an adoption plan

Semiopen adoption a style of adoption that involves the sharing of information (usually nonidentifying) between birth and adoptive parents through an intermediary

Special needs children see *Waiting children*

State reimbursements one-time financial assistance intended to help offset the expense of an adoption of a special needs child

State subsidies financial assistance intended to help offset ongoing expenses in caring for special needs children

Surrogacy the condition in which a woman carries and bears a child for another woman

Termination the legal conclusion of an adoption either before or after the adoption has been completed

Termination of parental rights the legal procedure that denies the birthparents any future claim to a child

Traditional adopters people who customarily fit a profile of an ideal adoptive parent: that is, white, under thirty-five, middle to upper class, two-parent families who were married over five years and who experience permanent infertility

Transcultural adoption in which the adopted children have a cultural heritage that differs from that of their adoptive parents

Transracial adoption in which the race of the adopted children differs from that of their adoptive parents

U.S. immigration laws federal laws governing the adoption of children internationally

GLOSSARY

Waiting children children who are frequently part of the interim care system and who are legally free for adoption
White any child of mainly European descent

SUGGESTED READING

Adoption and Infertility

Becker, Gay. *Healing the Infertile Family: Strengthening Your Relationship in the Search for Parenthood.* New York: Bantam Books, 1990.

Chase, Mary Earle. *Waiting for Baby: One Couple's Journey Through Infertility to Adoption.* New York: McGraw Hill, 1990.

Johnston, Patricia Irwin. *Adoption After Infertility: The Decision, the Commitment, the Experience.* Indianapolis: Perspectives Press, 1992.

General Adoption

olles, Edmund Blair. *The Penguin Adoption Handbook: A Guide to Creating Your New Family.* New York: Penguin ooks, 1993.

n, John. *Adoption in Canada.* Mississauga, Ontario: Counsel Press, 1993.

Lois. *The Adoption Resource Book.* New York: Perennial, 1992.

acqueline. *Successful Adoption: A Guide to a Child and Raising a Family.* New York: 987.

ed. *Adoption Without Fear.* San Antonio, ishing, 1989.

pen Adoption: A Caring Option.* Buena Glory Press, 1988.

Silber, Kathleen, and Phyllis Speedlin. *Dear Birthmother: Thank You for Our Baby.* San Antonio, TX: Corona Publishing, 1991.

How to Adopt

Adamec, Christine A. *How to Adopt Privately.* New York: Pinnacle Books, 1992.

Adamec, Christine A. *There ARE Babies to Adopt.* New York: Pinnacle Books, 1990.

Marindin, Hope, ed. *The Handbook for Single Adoptive Parents.* Chevy Chase, MD: Committee for Single Adoptive Parents, 1992.

Martin, Cynthia D. *Beating the Adoption Game.* New York: Harcourt, Brace, 1988.

International, Special Needs, and Older Children Adoptions

Jewett, Claudia L. *Adopting the Older Child.* Boston, MA: Harvard Common Press, 1978.

McNamara, Joan, and Bernard McNamara, eds. *Adoption and the Sexually Abused Child.* Portland, ME: University of Southern Maine, 1990.

Nelson-Erichsen, Jean, and Heino R. Erichsen. *How to Adopt Internationally.* Minneapolis: Dillon Press, 1992.

Parenting Adopted Children

Hallenbeck, Carol. *Our Child: Preparation for Parenting in Adoption.* Wayne, PA: Our Child Press, 1988.

Melina, Lois R. *Making Sense of Adoption: A Parent's Guide.* New York: HarperCollins, 1989.

Melina, Lois R. *Raising Adopted Children.* New York: Harper & Row, 1986.

Books for Adopted Children and Teens

Brodzinsky, Anne B. *The Mulberry Bird*. Indianapolis: Perspectives Press, 1986 (ages four to twelve).

Bunin, Catherine, and Sherry Bunin. *Is That Your Sister? A True Story of Adoption*. New York: Pantheon, 1992 (ages two to ten).

Fisher, Iris L. *Katie-Bo: An Adoption Story*. New York: Adama Books, 1988 (ages three to eight).

Freudberg, Judy, and Tony Geiss. *Susan and Gordon Adopt a Baby*. New York: Random Books Young Readers, 1992 (ages two to eight).

Kasza, Keiko. *A Mother for Choco*. New York: G. P. Putnam's Sons, 1992 (ages two to eight).

Kremetz, Jill. *How It Feels to Be Adopted*. New York: Knopf, 1982 (teens).

Rosenberg, Maxine B. *Growing Up Adopted*. New York: Bradbury Press, 1989 (teens).

Appendix A

ADOPTION ORGANIZATIONS

Adoptive Families of America
OURS: The Magazine of Adoptive Families
AFA
3333 Highway 100 North
Minneapolis, MN 55422
(612) 535-4829

Aask America—Adopt a Special Kid, America
registries of waiting children and prospective families
AASK
657 Mission Street
Suite 601
San Francisco, CA 94105
(415) 543-2275

Alliance of Genetic Support Groups
emphasis on genetic disorders
1001 22nd Street NW
Suite 800
Washington, DC 20037

(800) 336-GENE;
(202) 331-0942

American Academy of Adoption Attorneys
write for free directory
Box 33053
Washington, DC 20033-0053

American Adoption Congress
information for searching adult adoptees and birth-parents
AAC
Box 44040
L'Enfant Plaza Station
Washington, DC 20026

The CAP Book
publishes photolistings of waiting children
700 Exchange Street
Rochester, NY 14608
(716) 232-5110

Child Welfare League of America, Inc.
advocates for children
CWLA
440 First Street NW
Suite 310
Washington, DC 20001
(202) 638-2952

Committee for Single Adoptive Parents
The Handbook for Single Adoptive Parents
Box 15084
Chevy Chase, MD 20815

International Concerns Committee for Children
information service on adoptable domestic and international children
Report on Foreign Adoption
ICCC
911 Cypress Drive
Boulder, CO 80303
(303) 494-8333

National Adoption Center
general information, computer matching of waiting children and prospective families
1500 Walnut Street
Suite 701
Philadelphia, PA 19102
(800) TO-ADOPT

National Adoption Information Clearinghouse
wide range of free or inexpensive information
11426 Rockville Pike
Suite 410
Rockville, MD 20852
(301) 231-6512

National Association of Black Social Workers
advocates same-race adoptive placement of African-American children
15231 West McNichols
Detroit, MI 48235

National Committee for Adoption
general information on adoption
NCFA
1930 17th Street NW
Washington, DC 20009

National Resource Center for Special Needs Adoption
information about special needs adoption

APPENDIX A: ADOPTION ORGANIZATIONS

referrals to agencies with expertise in special needs adoption
Spaulding for Children
16250 Northland Drive
Suite 120
Southville, MI 48075
(313) 443-7080

North American Council on Adoptable Children
advocates for waiting children
Adoptalk
NACAC
1821 University Drive
Suite N-498
St. Paul, MN 55104
(612) 644-3036

RESOLVE, Inc.
infertility information and support network
1310 Broadway
Somerville, MA 02144
(617) 623-0744

Single Parents for Adoptive Children Everywhere
information for single parents and prospective adoptive singles
SPACE
6 Sunshine Avenue
Natick, MA 01760

CANADA

Adoption Council of Canada
Information and Education Services
Box 8442 Stn. T
Ottawa, Ontario K1G 3H8
(613) 235-1566

Adoption Council of Ontario
134 Clifton Road
Toronto, Ontario M4T 2G6
(416) 482-0021

Adoption Helper
newsletter
189 Springdale Boulevard
Toronto, Ontario M4C 1Z6
(416) 463-9412

Adoptive Parents Association of Alberta
parent support group member of Adoptive Families of America
Box 6496
Bonnyville, Alberta T9N 2H1
(403) 826-5625

Canadopt
networking for international and transracial adoptive families, especially developing nations
RR #3
Komoka, Ontario N0L 1P0
(519) 641-0796

Appendix B

STATE ADOPTION AGENCIES

ALABAMA
State Department of Human Resources
50 Ripley Street
Montgomery, AL 36130
(205) 242-9500

ALASKA
Department of Health and Social Services
Division of Family and Youth Services
P.O. Box H
Juneau, AK 99811-0630
(907) 465-3633

ARIZONA
Department of Economic Security
P.O. Box 6123
Site Code 940A
Phoenix, AZ 85005
(602) 542-2362

ARKANSAS
Department of Human Services
Division of Children and Family Services
P.O. Box 1437
Little Rock, AR 72203
(501) 682-8345

CALIFORNIA
Adoptions Branch
Department of Social Services
744 P Street
Sacramento, CA 95814
(916) 322-3778

COLORADO
Department of Social Services
1575 Sherman Street
Denver, CO 80203-1714
(303) 866-3209

APPENDIX B: STATE ADOPTION AGENCIES

CONNECTICUT
Department of Children and Youth Services
Connecticut Adoption Resource Exchange
Whitehall Building 2
Undercliff Road
Meridan, CT 06450
(203) 238-6640

DELAWARE
Adoption Services
1825 Faulkland Road
Wilmington, DE 19805-1195
(302) 633-2655

DISTRICT OF COLUMBIA
Department of Human Services
609 H Street NE
Washington, DC 20002
(202) 727-7226

FLORIDA
Department of Health and Rehabilitative Services
1317 Winewood
Building 8
Tallahassee, FL 32301
(904) 488-8000

GEORGIA
Department of Human Resources
Division of Family and Child Services
878 Peachtree NE, #501
Atlanta, GA 30309
(404) 894-3376

HAWAII
Department of Social Service
P.O. Box 339
Honolulu, HI 96809
(808) 548-6739

IDAHO
Department of Health and Welfare
450 West State Street
Boise, ID 83720
(208) 334-5697

ILLINOIS
Department of Children and Family Services
406 East Monroe
Springfield, IL 62701
For general information contact:
Adoption Information Center of Illinois

201 North Wells Street
Chicago, IL 60602
(312) 346-1516

INDIANA
Department of Public Welfare
Children and Family Services
  Division
402 West Washington Street
Room W364
Indianapolis, IN 46204
(317) 232-5613

IOWA
Adoption Program
Department of Human
  Services
Hoover Building
Des Moines, IA 50319
(515) 281-5358

KANSAS
Commission of Adult and
  Youth Services
Department of Social and
  Rehabilitation Services
300 S.W. Oakley
Topeka, KS 66606
(913) 296-4661

KENTUCKY
Cabinet for Human
  Resources
Department for Social
  Services
275 East Main Street
Frankfort, KY 40621
(502) 564-2136

LOUISIANA
Office of Community
  Services/Children, Youth
  and Family
1967 North Street
Baton Rouge, LA 70821
(504) 342-4086

MAINE
Department of Human
  Services
221 State Street
Augusta, ME 04333
(207) 289-5060

MARYLAND
Family and Children's
  Services
Social Services
  Administration
311 West Saratoga Street
Baltimore, MD 21201
(301) 333-0236

MASSACHUSETTS
Department of Social
  Services

24 Fannsworth Street
Boston, MA 02110
(617) 727-0900

MICHIGAN
Department of Social
　Services
P.O. Box 30037
Lansing, MI 48909
(517) 373-3513

MINNESOTA
Department of Human
　Services
444 Lafayette Road
St. Paul, MN 55155
(612) 296-0584

MISSISSIPPI
Department of Human
　Services
Adoption Unit
P. O. Box 352
Jackson, MS 39205
(601) 354-0341

MISSOURI
Division of Family Services
Department of Social
　Services
P.O. Box 88
Jefferson City, MO 65103
(314) 751-2882

MONTANA
Department of Family
　Services
Box 8005
Helena, MT 59604
(406) 444-5900

NEBRASKA
Department of Social
　Services
301 Centennial Mall South
Lincoln, NE 68509
(402) 471-9331

NEVADA
Division of Child and Family
　Services
700 Belrose Street
Las Vegas, NV 89158
(702) 486-5270

NEW HAMPSHIRE
Division for Children and
　Youth Services
6 Hazen Drive
Concord, NH 03301
(603) 271-4721

NEW JERSEY
Division of Youth and Family
　Services
Adoption Unit
CN 717

1 South Montgomery Street
Trenton, NJ 08625-0717
(609) 633-6902

NEW MEXICO
Department of Human
 Services
P.O. Box 2348
Santa Fe, NM 87504
(505) 827-8423

NEW YORK
Department of Social
 Services
Adoption Services
40 North Pearl Street
Albany, NY 12243
(800) 345-KIDS

NORTH CAROLINA
Division of Social Services
325 North Salisbury Street
Raleigh, NC 27603
(919) 733-3801

NORTH DAKOTA
Children and Family Services
Department of Human
 Services
600 East Boulevard Avenue
Bismarck, ND 58505-0250
(701) 224-4811

OHIO
Department of Human
 Services
Adoptions
65 East State Street
Columbus, OH 43266
(800) 686-1581 or
 (614) 466-9274

OKLAHOMA
Department of Human
 Services
P.O. Box 25352
Oklahoma City, OK 73125
(405) 521-2475

OREGON
Adoption Services
Children's Services
 Division
198 Commercial Street SE
Salem, OR 97310
(503) 378-4121

PENNSYLVANIA
Department of Public
 Welfare
Office of Children, Youth and
 Families
P.O. Box 2675
Harrisburg, PA 17105-2675
(717) 257-7003

RHODE ISLAND
Department for Children and
  Their Families
610 Mt. Pleasant Avenue
Providence, RI 02908
(401) 457-4654

SOUTH CAROLINA
Department of Social Services
Division of Adoption and
  Birth Parent Services
P.O. Box 1520
Columbia, SC 29202
(803) 734-6095

SOUTH DAKOTA
Child Protection Services
Department of Social Services
700 Governors Drive
Pierre, SD 57501
(605) 773-3227

TENNESSEE
Department of Human
  Services
400 Deaderick Street
Nashville, TN 37248-9000
(615) 741-5935

TEXAS
Department of Human
  Services
P.O. Box 149030
Austin, TX 78714-9030
(512) 450-3302

UTAH
Division of Family Services
120 North 200 West
Salt Lake City, UT 84103
(801) 538-4080

VERMONT
Social and Rehabilitation
  Services
103 South Main Street
Waterbury, VT 05676
(802) 241-2131

VIRGINIA
Department of Social
  Services
Bureau of Child Welfare
  Services
8007 Discovery Drive
Richmond, VA 23229
(804) 662-9025

WASHINGTON
Division of Children and
  Family Services
P.O. Box 45713/OB41
Olympia, WA 98504
(206) 753-2178

WEST VIRGINIA
Department of Health and
   Human Resources
Bureau of Human Resources
Office of Social Services
State Capitol Complex
Building 6
Charleston, WV 25305
(304) 348-7980

WISCONSIN
Department of Health and
   Social Services
Division of Community
   Services
P.O. Box 7851
Madison, WI 53707-7851
(608) 266-0690

WYOMING
Department of Family
   Services
319 Hathaway Building
2300 Capitol Avenue
Cheyenne, WY 82002
(307) 777-7561

CANADA
National Adoption Desk
Health and Welfare Canada
Room 1201, Finance Bldg.
Tunney's Pasture
Ottawa, Ontario K1A 1B5
(613) 952-6117

MANITOBA
Director of Programs
Family Services–Child and
   Family Support
Department of Family Services,
   2nd Floor
114 Garry Street
Winnipeg, Manitoba R3C 1G1
(204) 945-6964

ONTARIO
Adoption Unit
Ministry of Community & Social
   Services
2 Bloor Street W, 24th Floor
Toronto, Ontario M7A 1E9
(416) 327-4730

PRINCE EDWARD ISLAND
Co-ordinator, Child in Care
Department of Health & Social
   Services
P.O. Box 2000
Charlottestown, P.E.I.
   C1A 7N8
(902) 368-4931

SASKATCHEWAN
Adoption Services
Family and Youth Services
Saskatchewan Social Services
12th Floor
1920 Broad Street
Regina, Saskatchewan S4P 3V7
(306) 787-5698

INDEX

Abortion, 20
Abused child, 139
Adopted child
  easing transition of, 138–140
Adoption. *See also* Legal process
  and supply and demand, 20–21
  changes in, 25–26
  confidential, 28–29, 55–57
  difficulty of, 18–19
  issues related to, 8–12, 147
  open, 29, 55–57
  requirements for, 33–34, 37
  safeguards in, 68–74
  semiopen, 29, 55–57
  styles of, 49–59
  tips for success in, 129–131
Adoption agencies, 52–53
  services of, 81–82, 125–126
Adoption agents, 53–54
  services of, 81–82, 125–126
Adoption laws
  principle of "best interest of the child," 24
  protective legislation, 22–23
Adoption organizations, 181–183
Adoption plan, 36–37
Adoption strategy, 75
  choosing a professional, 80–84
  six-step plan, 76–79
Adoption support groups, 13–15
Adoptive Families of America, 13, 67

Adoptive parents. *See also* Prospective parents
  adjustments of, 134–137
  choices of, 25
  profile of, 33
Advertising, 91, 96–101
  classified, 110–117
  flyers, 104–106
  mailings, 107–109
  networking, 102–103
Attorneys, 53

Barriers to adoption, 18–19
Benefits, 142
Birth control, 20
Birth defects, 152–153
Birthmother, 8–9, 11
  adoption plan of, 36–37
  advertising for, 96–101
  and open adoption, 56–57
  changes of heart, 69, 71, 95, 150–152
  choices of, 25
  expanding role of, 30–31
  initial communication with, 121–126
  locating, 90–101
  meeting with, 128–129
  profile of typical, 97–99, 127
  qualities in adoptive parents sought after, 127–128
Bonding, 72, 146–149

Books on adoption, 140, 178–180

Changes in adoption practices, 25–26
Changes of heart, 69, 71, 95, 150–152
Children of color, 41–42
Classified advertising, 110–117
  advantages of, 113
  disadvantages of, 113
  patterning, 113–114
  successes and failures of, 118–120
  ten tips for success, 114–117
Confidential adoption, 27–29, 55–57
Contingency plan, 78–79, 85–87
Costs of adoption, 37, 52–53
Counseling, 71–74, 128, 138–139
Cultural background, 139

Decision to adopt, 1–2, 8–12
Defense Authorization Bill of 1991, 143
Difficulty of adoption, 18–19
Disappointment
  birth defects, 152–153
  birthmother decides to parent, 150–152
  disruption and dissolution, 152
Disruption, 152
Dissolution, 152
Doctors, 53
Domestic adoption, 58–59
Domestic white infants, 36–37

Entitlement, 146–149

Family and friends, 15–17
Family preparation, 134–137

Feminism, 20
Financial assistance, 142–143
Financial information, 83
Flyers, 104–106
Foster care children, 43–45
Fraud, 68, 71

Glossary, 172–177
Grandparents, 135–137
Grieving process, 72

Hague Convention on Inter-Country Adoption, 66
Health insurance, 141
Home study, 62
Home visits, 63
Hospital staffs, 89

Identified adoption, 92
Incomplete records, 10
Indian Child Welfare Act of 1978, 42
Infertile couples, 21
  losses of, 5–7
  options of, 3–4
Interim care children, 43–45
International adoption, 58–59, 67
International children, 38–40
Interstate adoptions, 66
Interstate Compact on the Placement of Children, 65–66, 74

Jurisdiction, 65–66

Laws of adoption, 22–24
  international regulations, 38–39
Lawyers, 53
Legal documentation, 82–83

INDEX

Legal process, 60
  international adoptions, 67
  interstate adoption, 66
  jurisdiction, 65–66
  procedures, 63–64
  regulations, 61–63
  safeguards in, 68–74
Legal risk adoptions (fost/adopt), 44
Legal system, 18–19
Life book, 139

Mailings, 107–109
Medical records, 83, 135
Milestones, 144–145
Military benefits, 143

National Association of Black Social Workers, 10
Native American children, 42
Negativity, 11, 89
Networking, 102–103
Nontraditional parents, 34, 157–168
North American Council on Adoptable Children, 13–15

Omnibus Budget Reconciliation Act of 1993, 141
Open adoption, 29, 55–57
Openness in adoption, 27–29

Parent support groups, 13–15
Parent-initiated adoptions, 90–95
Personal data, 83
Physical differences, 9–10
Positive adoption language, 154–156
Prejudice, 9–10, 42
Private adoption agencies, 53

Procedures, 63–64
Professionals, 80–84
Prospective parents
  new options for, 31–32
Protective legislation, 22–23
Public adoption agencies, 52

Questions for birthmother, 122–123

Records
  incomplete, 10
Regulations, 61–63
Requirements for adoption, 33–34, 37
Resumes, 107–109
Reversals, 62–63
Risks, 88–89

Safeguards, 68–74
Semiopen adoption, 29, 55–57
Sibling group, 71
Siblings, 135–137
Social service agencies, 52
Societal changes, 20–21
Special needs children, 46–48, 71
State adoption agencies, 184–190
State laws, 74
Stresses, 88–89, 138
Styles of adoption, 49–50
  adoption agencies, 52–53
  adoption agents, 53–54
  confidential, semiopen, or open, 55–57
  domestic or international, 58–59
Subsidies, 142–143
Supply and demand, 20–21
Support systems
  adoption support groups, 13–15

    family and friends, 15–17
    informal, 13
    structured, 13

Termination of parental rights, 63
Traditional adopter's profile, 33
Transracial/transcultural
    adoption, 9–10, 41–42

Waiting children, 46–48, 71

Waiting times, 37, 39, 52–53
Weekly shoppers, 111
White infants, 36–37
Who can adopt, 33–34
Who can be adopted, 35
    children of color, 41–42
    domestic white infants, 36–37
    foster care children, 43–45
    international children, 38–40
    waiting children, 46–48

PARENTING KEYS JUST FOR PARENTS AND PARENTS-TO-BE!

Keys to...

- Adopting a Child
- Anxious Child
- Becoming a Father
- Breast Feeding
- Calming the Fussy Baby
- Child Safety and Care of Minor Injuries
- Childhood Illnesses
- Children's Nutrition
- Children's Sleep Problems
- Choosing Childcare
- Dealing with Childhood Allergies
- Dealing with Stuttering
- Disciplining Your Young Child
- Investing in Your Child's Future
- Parenting a Child with a Learning Disability
- Parenting a Child with Attention Deficit Disorder
- Parenting a Child with Down Syndrome
- Parenting an Adopted Child
- Parenting the Asthmatic Child
- Parenting the Child with Autism
- Parenting the Gifted Child
- Parenting Twins
- Parenting Your Five-Year-Old
- Parenting Your One-Year-Old
- Parenting Your Teenager
- Parenting Your Three-Year-Old
- Parenting Your Two-Year-Old
- Preparing and Caring for Your Newborn
- Preparing and Caring for Your Second Child
- Single Parenting
- Successful Music Lessons
- Successful Stepmothering
- Teaching Children About God

Each Key: Paperback, $5.95 & $6.95 (Canada $7.95 & $8.95)

Books may be purchased at your bookstore, or by mail from Barron's. Enclose check or money order for total amount plus sales tax where applicable and 15% for postage and handling (minimum charge $4.95). Prices are subject to change without notice.

(#39) R 3/97

Barron's Educational Series, Inc.
250 Wireless Boulevard
Hauppauge, NY 11788
Call toll free: 1-800-645-3476

POTTY-TRAINING RELIEF FOR PARENTS AND KIDS!

ONCE UPON A POTTY *Is Now a Package Deal!*

Once Upon A Potty—The Package, by Alona Frankel, includes the best-selling book, an 8-inch tall, stuffed fabric doll equipped with plastic potty, and a 30-minute animated music video filled with humor, expert advice, and successful toilet-training techniques. Comic relief for parents and fun for kids, these colorful packages encourage parents and children to laugh, sing, and learn together! (Ages 1–4 and their parents)
Each Package: 10"W × 11"H × 6½"D

HER VERSION: ISBN: 0-8120-7765-2, $26.95, Canada $33.95

HIS VERSION: ISBN: 0-8120-7764-4, $28.95, Canada $35.95

Books may be purchased at your bookstore, or by mail from Barron's. Enclose check or money order for the total amount plus sales tax where applicable and 15% for postage and handling charge (minimum charge $4.95). Prices are subject to change without notice.

Barron's Educational Series, Inc.
250 Wireless Boulevard
Hauppauge, NY 11788

IN CANADA:
Georgetown Book Warehouse
34 Armstrong Avenue
Georgetown, Ontario L7G 4R9

(#38) R 11/96